Screwed

Screwed

How Women Are
Set Up to Fail at Sex

LILI BOISVERT

Translated by Arielle Aaronson

DUNDURN
TORONTO

Printer: Webcom, a division of Marquis Book Printing, Inc.

Library and Archives Canada Cataloguing in Publication

Boisvert, Lili, 1985-
[Principe du cumshot. English]
    Screwed : how women are set up to fail at sex / Lili Boisvert ; translated by Arielle Aaronson.

Translation of: Le principe du cumshot.
Includes bibliographical references.
Issued in print and electronic formats.
ISBN 978-1-4597-4357-1 (softcover).--ISBN 978-1-4597-4358-8 (PDF).--ISBN 978-1-4597-4359-5 (EPUB)

    1. Women--Sexual behaviour. 2. Sexual instinct. 3. Sexual freedom. I. Aaronson, Arielle, translator II. Title. II. Title: Principe du cumshot. English

HQ29.B6413 2019   306.7082   C2018-906009-3
                                              C2018-906010-7

1 2 3 4 5   23   22   21 20 19

 Conseil des Arts du Canada   Canada Council for the Arts   Canada   ONTARIO ARTS COUNCIL / CONSEIL DES ARTS DE L'ONTARIO   Québec Production Services Tax Credit SODEC

The translation was realized with the financial support of the **Société de développement des entreprises culturelles** (SODEC).

We acknowledge the support of the **Canada Council for the Arts**, which last year invested $153 million to bring the arts to Canadians throughout the country, and the **Ontario Arts Council** for our publishing program. We also acknowledge the financial support of the **Government of Ontario**, through the **Ontario Book Publishing Tax Credit** and **Ontario Creates**, and the **Government of Canada**.

Nous remercions le **Conseil des arts du Canada** de son soutien. L'an dernier, le Conseil a investi 153 millions de dollars pour mettre de l'art dans la vie des Canadiennes et des Canadiens de tout le pays.

Dundurn
VISIT US AT

   dundurn.com | @dundurnpress | dundurnpress | dundurnpress

3 Church Street, Suite 500
Toronto, Ontario, Canada
M5E 1M2

Contents

Warning   7

Introduction: What's Left to   11
Say About Sex?

1   Me Hunter, You Prey: Passivity as the   15
Cornerstone of Femininity

2   Cougars and Nymphets: Glorifying the   40
Younger Woman

3   The Purity Imperative: Innocence —   59
the Essence of the Slut

4   Sex Segregation: From Objectification to   75
Autophilia

5   The First Sex: Teaching Women Not to   100
Objectify Men

6   The Holy Grail: Heterosexual Sex and   114
Psychological Treats

7   The Orgasm Gap: Aim for the G Spot and   136
Miss the Target

Conclusion: Rethinking Sex to   159
Liberate Women

The Cumshot Principle Flow Chart   165

Glossary   166

Notes   169

Warning

This book is about sex — more specifically, about female desire. But it might not be quite what you expect.

I know from experience (after all, I've often been labelled a sex maniac because of what I do) that when it comes to sex, people have a lot of preconceived notions. And since I don't want to be accused of false advertising, let's set a few things straight.

THIS BOOK IS NOT:

1. Advocating that women "explore their sexuality" further

Although this book is about female desire, I will not urge women to boost their libido by experimenting more in bed. I will not tell them to go buy sexy lingerie so they "feel like a woman." I will not describe how to give the world's best blowjob — after all, how would I know?

2. A guide for men

If you are looking for advice on how to find your partner's (or partners') G spot, you will be disappointed. And the same goes for men looking for tricks to pick up women — again, how would I know?

3. An anti-man manifesto

Some men might feel attacked as they read this book, but my work isn't about men or their behaviour. It isn't even about female behaviour, so to speak. Rather, this book focuses on relationships between men and women.

4. A book for couples, or people looking for love

This book is not aimed at couples hoping to spice up their sex life, or at singles looking for a relationship. On the contrary, it is a universal exploration of human sexuality.

THIS BOOK IS:

1. Western-centric

The book will look at Western perceptions of sex. Some of my arguments may very well apply to other regions of the world, but I will limit my work to the culture I know and avoid drawing universal conclusions.

2. Heterosexual in focus

This book is first and foremost about cisgender heterosexual relations. The idea is not to dismiss or invalidate homosexual or bisexual relations or relations of members of the transgender community, but I will be focusing on relations between cis men and women, as they constitute the dominant model of sex on which our culture is built.

3. A critical reflection on sex

These pages contain a critical analysis of how sexual clichés influence our collective behaviours, and how they affect and shape women's desire, depriving them of their autonomy.

Introduction

What's Left to Say About Sex?

I get this question a lot, and I can understand why. Given the abundant literature written about sex, its omnipresence on screens all around us, and the billions of porn videos we have access to, you might think we've exhausted the subject — yet the reality is, we've barely scratched the surface.

I believe the sexual revolution that began in the 1960s came to an abrupt halt, and we're still living in the world that produced it. Women's sexual liberation, one of feminism's key platforms, never came to fruition — all we had was a brief taste.

Sure, we're probably talking more about sex today than we did before, but only on a superficial level. The media tend to take a condescending approach to the subject. It is treated lightly, using comedy, or as a strictly biological affair, but rarely discussed in terms of its relevance or importance to society as a whole. So many questions are left unresolved or get brushed aside with simplistic answers.

Why do we have sex? What attracts us to other people? Why are our fantasies so similar? Why do we adopt certain behaviours in bed rather than others? And why do we have such specific expectations when it comes to the dynamics of seduction between a man and a woman?

Most theories centre on the notion that when it comes to sex, the way things are currently is necessary and unchangeable. Why do we prefer women with large breasts and a slim waist? Because they're more fertile. Why are men so driven by a desire to have sex? Because of testosterone.

By blaming biology, we ignore the fact that humans — social creatures by nature — are influenced by a range of environmental factors. These explanations sidestep the richness and complexity of human motivations.

But it's these simplistic answers that abound in popular culture. And we cling to them, because they validate our current choices and behaviours.

Another reason we accept these answers is because our relationship to sexuality remains mysterious in many ways. We like to believe that our sexuality springs from a deep and primal place within us, a realm governed by magical hormonal urges that overwhelm our minds and bodies. We are at the mercy of these cravings, having done nothing to fuel them. They strike us in a flash — poof!

We talk a lot about sex. But we talk about it as if it's the great joke at the heart of human nature or to justify our behaviours, not to engage in a deeper reflection.

The truth is, we don't actually want to understand our sexual mores. And above all, we refuse to acknowledge that the rules governing our sexual culture are used to repress women. We ignore the fact that our customs and rituals mainly serve to police women's desire, so that it adapts to the desire we feel *toward* women. From this perspective, the female libido becomes a tool for social control.

It's time to get our heads out of the sand, temper the hormone talk, and realize there is nothing natural, necessary, or immutable in the sexist clichés we impose on women's libido.

Female desire has been hacked — diverted from women's own interests by what I call the "cumshot principle."

1

Me Hunter, You Prey:
Passivity as the Cornerstone of Femininity

> Being a sex symbol is a
> heavy load to carry.
> — Marilyn Monroe

As unsexy as it might seem, sex is highly codified. It is a social activity, and like all social activities, it involves specific ways of interacting with each other.

In other words, sex is a matter of tradition.

And since our sexual traditions tend not to be discussed or studied — and therefore questioned — we are all the more conformist when we engage in them.

This conformity is apparent from the first moments of the heterosexual encounter. Women and men have traditionally adopted clearly defined roles based on what is expected from both sides. These roles are supposed to be complementary (we love to think of everything related to heterosexual sexuality as complementary!) and highly differentiated. Things are black and white: man is a hunter, and woman is his prey. The result is an active/passive relationship. This is the first component of the cumshot principle.

In pornography, the "cumshot" is the moment when the camera captures a man ejaculating onto a woman's body or face. It is the final scene, and leaves the actress covered in sperm.

This image is a perfect representation of the principle underlying a typical heterosexual relationship: in our dominant conception of sexuality, desire originates with the man and is directed upon the woman.

And that is the cumshot principle.

Female passivity is a direct consequence of this principle: the woman acts as a target, and a target is passive. The person launching the projectile is active, while the target's defining function is to receive the object.

This principle comes into play as soon as the man and woman enter the seduction phase.

As a society, we have decided that women embody sex. A woman fundamentally "possesses" sex within her. We have also decided that men, who do not embody sex — and therefore do not possess it — must convince women to give sex to them. Which means that a woman must give *herself* to a man.

The rules of conduct I am about to describe are stereotypes. This is intentional. They are our ideals, the male and female behaviours we expect. Certainly, there are thousands of situations where these rules don't apply, but the behavioural patterns they create have a powerful influence on our relationships. Even if we don't always adopt them, violating them makes us uncomfortable, makes us fear judgment. Most of the time we abide by these rules without thinking, whether out of habit, imitation, or because the price to pay for defying them is too high.

Let's look at how these ideals are manifested during a heterosexual encounter.

THE MAN'S ROLE

1. Make the first move

The man plays the active role during seduction. It is his responsibility to approach the woman. The man is expected to begin by complimenting her or striking up a conversation, which he must sustain. It also falls to him to ask for the first date.

During this time, the woman must hold the man's interest while remaining relatively passive. She shouldn't take the lead and must curb her enthusiasm or risk appearing desperate. Or aggressive. Or obsessed. Think Samantha Jones in *Sex and the City*.

Samantha's character claims to embody the "liberated woman," yet she is the only one to initiate romantic encounters; Carrie, Miranda, and Charlotte display classic passive behaviour with men. Far from the typical representation of a modern woman, Samantha is an anomaly, and shockingly so. She is a kind of anti-hero of seduction. Samantha serves as a counterexample that underscores just how unusual it is for a woman to act this way (which creates a comic effect).

Getting back to the classic scenario: a man who makes the first move doesn't seem desperate, intense, or obsessed. He is behaving as we would expect any "normal" man to behave. To be considered aggressive, he would have to become very persistent in the event of a rejection.

2. Amuse and entertain

Women do not expect men to seduce them with their bodies. As a result, men can get away with being much less concerned about their appearance. Of course, men

WHAT ABOUT THE NEXT GENERATION?

You might think that this active male/passive female dynamic is a thing of the past, more applicable to our grandparents' generation. While it's true that the blurring of these roles is not as shocking as it once was, the majority of us — teenagers included — still adhere to them in practice. The basic picture remains as topical as ever.

In a course given by American sociologist Paula England on relations between men and women on university campuses, 75 percent of students surveyed said it was acceptable for a woman to make the first move.[1] Yet almost all of them reported that in reality, it is men who initiate an encounter. Young people therefore accept the notion of a female hunter/male prey in theory, but this is not reflected in their behaviour. Judging something to be appropriate doesn't mean we embrace it as so with our actions.

are judged on their looks, but a man's body is not usually a deal-breaker when it comes to attracting a woman.

Men can often compensate for an average physique with a sharp sense of humour or a good reputation, by being cultured or having impressive knowledge, by possessing significant financial resources or having prestige associated with certain jobs. These attributes won't garner the same sex appeal for an average-looking woman.

From this wide selection of criteria, women also frequently cite a sense of humour as being important in a mate.

Indeed, humour plays a major role in courtship; both men and women claim to look for this quality in a partner. However, studies have shown that the genders are actually talking about different things. A woman looking for a "sense of humour" wants a man who makes jokes and who likes to laugh. A man looking for the same quality in a woman does not expect her to be funny; rather, he wants her to laugh at his own jokes.[2]

Jeffrey Hall, University of Kansas researcher and author of a 2015 study on humour, believes this difference in meaning reflects the everyday sexism[3] that influences the dynamics of courtship.[4]

Hall argues that the way heterosexuals express humour is connected to the traditional roles attributed to each gender: "Humour production during courtship could be interpreted as a sign of dominance and laughter in response to a sign of submissiveness."

According to Hall, the man performs for the woman, who is his receptive audience. The active/passive dynamic is once again at play.

We observe the same phenomenon when it comes to communication skills. According to a recent study conducted by the University of Buffalo's Department of Communication, women find men who are good at storytelling sexier than men who are not. Men, however, tend to be indifferent regarding this talent in women.[5]

3. Initiate and direct sexual relations

It is also the man's responsibility to set the sexual encounter in motion.

In fact, if the woman in a couple tries to initiate sex, her desire and advances may go unnoticed. According to three studies conducted by the University of Toronto and the University of Western Ontario[6] in 2016, men have a hard time determining when their partners are in the mood for sex, while women are well attuned to the signs in their male partners. The signals men send are therefore perceived far better than those sent by women.

When a sexual encounter is under way, men are expected to maintain control. Like dominant Christian in *Fifty Shades of Grey*. Or like men who toss women this way and that in porn films.

This imperative is also reflected in our language. A man "takes" a woman. A woman "gives herself" to a man, "yielding" to his advances, whereupon he "possesses her."

Or consider the verb *to screw*, often used to designate a sexual encounter. The term can be used by both sexes: "I want to screw him," "I screwed her," etc. But if we reflect on the verb's principal meaning, *to screw* places the emphasis on the implement; the tool itself joins two objects together. This brings us back to the prescribed roles for both genders: the man actively unites the two bodies by inserting his penis into the woman's vagina. The man screws; the woman is screwed.

When we talk about penetration, we are referencing just that: the act of penetrating. It is the man who penetrates the woman and not, for example, the woman who pleasures the man or who shoves the man's penis into her vagina. But why? If the woman is on top throughout sex, she is clearly the one acting on the man's penis. If the man remains motionless while the woman grinds her body against his, again, she is the acting force. But do we ever use this language to talk about a vagina and penis interacting? No. That would mean giving the woman an active role, an idea that makes us uncomfortable.

THE WOMAN'S ROLE

1. Make her body as attractive as possible

Although women don't anticipate seduction will rely on a man's looks, men expect to be seduced by a woman's appearance. While it is certainly not the only thing they take into account, it is the first element they are drawn to consider — a hunter's first step is to choose his prey. And how does he choose? By selecting the "best" potential targets according to current standards of beauty.

From a young age, women learn that their physical appearance plays a fundamental role in determining their value as a human being. Consequently, they come to take great care in maintaining their image. The pressure to be beautiful comes at them from all sides: fashion, makeup products, hair dyes, plastic surgery, and so on. Though we may claim that men are equally preoccupied by their appearance, the numbers don't lie: women are the largest consumers of fashion and beauty products.

This imperative is a matter of objectification. The disproportionate amount of attention we place on a woman's physical appearance automatically consigns her to the role of object during courtship. For a woman to be seduced by a man's personality, sense of humour, prestige, wealth, or intelligence, she must first get to know him. She will have to talk to him, ask him questions, and treat him like a whole and complex human being. As a hunter, a man doesn't need to do the same. A physique that meets his standards of attractiveness will often suffice to pique his sexual interest — personality is far outweighed by desire.

This double standard is at the core of the mass objectification of women. A woman deemed desirable can be two-dimensional, while a man must have a certain amount of depth.

2. Fend off unwanted advances

As we have seen, men initiate the courtship process. Women, as the object of male attention, must decide if they are willing to be courted. Perhaps they weren't in "seduction mode" when initially approached; a woman who is walking down the street when she is stopped by a stranger probably isn't looking for a romantic encounter. Yet frequently, men immediately

WHAT WE SAY AND WHAT WE DO

Fortunately, the prescribed rules for the type of heterosexual encounter described in this chapter aren't always followed to the letter. And it's interesting to note there can be a real disparity between conforming to stereotypes in theory and unconsciously displaying different behaviour in practice. In a 2008 study, psychology researchers in Illinois asked members of both genders (168 single students, approximately twenty years old) what they look for most in a potential partner. The men claimed to value physical appearance while the women valued a partner's wealth.[7] The study seemed to confirm the stereotypes; men like pretty women and women like rich men. But interestingly, when participants were put in real-life situations during a speed-dating session, things looked quite different. Faced with an opportunity to spend more time with the people they had enjoyed meeting earlier, participants reported attractiveness and wealth of the potential partners as equally important. There was no observable difference between genders. "People may lack introspective awareness of what influences their judgments and behaviour," concluded the researchers.

It seems, then, that the stereotypes we think we conform to don't always match up with the complexity of our motivations. All the more reason we should question these stereotypes, which set expectations and inform our choices.

perceive a woman they consider sexy and attractive to be in seduction mode (which is, of course, a passive mode for her). The man's logic might look something like: "I find you attractive, therefore you willingly provoked this reaction; you seduced me, which is a green light." In the eyes of the man, the decision to approach said woman is thus perfectly justified, and bound to be welcome.

This is why many men will get angry if the object of their attention rejects or ignores them. Obviously, no one likes to be rejected. But in the context of predatory courtship, male anger goes beyond the unpleasantness of rejection. It becomes a mixture of disappointment and feeling as though an injustice has been committed. The man is rejected *even though he was certain* he met the woman's expectations by approaching her. The least she can do is show some gratitude! He believes he has acknowledged efforts made by the seductress (as he perceives them) and that she should be receptive. He has validated her role as prey, so why on earth won't she return the validation of his role as active hunter?

Owing to their role as prey, it falls on women to fend off undesired advances and live with the hostility that sometimes results.

Men experience rejection more often than women when it comes to courtship, since they are usually the ones making the first move. The woman plays a semi-active role after the fact, by saying yes or no.

But what happens in shorter- or longer-term relationships, when the parties involved have differing views on the nature of the relationship? This is where the notion of the "friend zone" comes into play. This term refers to complaints typically voiced by a man who wants to have sex with a woman, though she is only looking to be friends. While he is aware of her sexual disinterest, the man pursues her in the hopes of changing her mind. He believes he will be able to convince her to sleep with him if he is patient and persistent enough. The idea here is that even if a woman hasn't openly attempted courtship, it doesn't mean she is not interested — and therefore the man should not give up. The woman's inaction should be taken simply as a passive and latent potential for sex.

3. Fend off wanted advances

Paradoxically, women are also expected to fend off the advances of men they *are* interested in.

We expect a "good" woman to give off hints of sensuality while remaining within the limits of modesty. As prey, her body should be put on display — but there's a fine line between appropriate female charm and the disapproval that comes from exposing the tiniest bit too much.

We use the terms "elegant" or "classy" to refer to a woman who is attractive yet stays within the limits of "good taste." And these limits are ambiguous. When is a low neckline too low? What is the right way to wear leggings? How much makeup is appropriate? There is no universal rule of good taste. Styles change over the years according to fashion trends, and even differ depending on who you ask. But one thing is certain: a woman who pushes the envelope too far will be severely judged.

Similarly, a woman whose sexual conduct is considered too brazen or forward will be punished. If her behaviour is not respectable, we might say she doesn't deserve to be respected.

Even within a dating context, a woman who accepts a sexual proposition too quickly — or one who initiates sex — runs the risk of being seen by men as a nymphomaniac[8] or a girl who shouldn't be taken seriously: good for a roll in the hay, but not "girlfriend material."

Women face yet another problem when they start falling for a man: for certain skilled hunters, the fun is in the chase. These men find it exciting when their prey resists for a while.

Women therefore end up with a social duty to fend off a man's initial advances — even when they are wanted.

4. Do not resist wanted and unwanted advances

Finally, to add another layer of confusion, we also expect women *not to resist* a man's sexual advances, either wanted or unwanted. Our culture considers it a woman's duty to remain sexually available. We have even coined terms to humiliate women who thwart men who want sex: *(cock)tease, flirt, temptress.*

I already talked about street harassment and how certain men get angry if women aren't receptive to their advances. And each time the issue is raised by the media, it's fascinating to see just how many women rush to defend male conduct. They consider it a question of seduction, not harassment. Like the men who pursue them, these women believe every woman should enjoy being approached on the street, should feel grateful to receive compliments from total strangers. They want that kind of validation, and buy into the idea that a woman shouldn't resent these advances or, at the very least, should deflect them by offering a gracious smile instead of acting annoyed, scared, indifferent, or angry.

What's more — and this is particularly disturbing — statistics for sexual assault by men against women[9] show that consent is often deemed superfluous in heterosexual interactions. Unfortunately, all too often, resistance from a woman is not judged by the aggressor to be a valid response.

5. Gasp, scream, and grimace in bed

One of society's expectations is that women should make noise and contort their faces during sex. In porn, as in real life, women shriek and moan enthusiastically and for extended periods, while men remain impassive, silent participants.

This is a ritual, a learned behaviour, which is even consciously adopted in certain cases. But surprisingly, many men — and women, for that matter — believe it to be an instinctive, uncontrollable reaction. It's comical, in a way, to see a woman masturbating on television: she inevitably makes noise and contorts her face into elaborate demonstrations of pleasure. Yet any woman who has ever masturbated knows that such a performance would be ridiculous if there were nobody to witness it.

Expressions of pleasure through sound and facial expressions may involve a measure of spontaneity, but there's no reason they should be more common among women than men. We see and hear women climaxing because it is an integral part of the passive role they have

"WE CAN'T EVEN HIT ON
WOMEN ANYMORE"

When women complain about the sexual harassment they face, they are frequently accused of wanting to eliminate all games of seduction between the sexes.

The unfortunate reason for this is that many people can't tell the difference between harassment and flirting. To clarify the terms, ask yourself the following: Is the person making the advances looking for signs of *reciprocity*?

When a man approaches a woman, is he checking to make sure she feels comfortable? Is he ready to stop the moment she indicates she is uneasy, annoyed, or unwilling to pursue the interaction (e.g., by ignoring him)?

If he is flirting, the man may hope that the interaction will be reciprocal, but he can recognize when it's time to humbly admit defeat — without getting angry or insulting the woman.

A man guilty of harassment doesn't necessarily care how the woman responds. His goal is to intimidate, to impose advances without considering whether or not they are welcome. He may think flagging a woman down on the street is a simple demonstration of masculinity, or that the woman owes him a positive response.

been assigned. Women must go into "reaction mode" when they're in bed. They have to communicate their pleasure — whether real, exaggerated, or completely fabricated — to encourage the man. In so doing, the woman allows her partner to maintain his silent arousal so he can focus on the deed without having to put on a show.

This practice is a good example of how women are perceived as passive beings that are acted upon by men. A woman must moan and cry out to show the man that she likes *what he is doing to her.*

If women had played a more active role during sex throughout history, men would have made much more noise in bed. The two genders would have met somewhere in the middle.

HOW CLICHÉS OF COURTSHIP IMPACT A WOMAN'S LIBIDO

Since men play the active role in heterosexual courtship rituals, women's sexual tension is dependent upon them. The female libido lies dormant as she waits for a potential partner to prove he is worthy of her interest. He must be deserving for her to "give" herself to him. Men make the first move, so it is up to them to prove their worth.

Because women do not make the first move, they don't get to choose their partner. They are chosen by a man. This means that whereas the man is clearly interested in the woman, she may not be particularly interested in her suitor at first.

(I'm curious to see if dating apps like Tinder, where users select each other — swipe right! — will reduce men's privilege as hunters in the future. But based on my observations so far, it appears that we stick to traditional behaviours once the match is made.)

Clearly, if a woman doesn't care for a man's physical appearance, she is unlikely to desire him at first. But she might remain open to the idea of being won over by his personality. Is he charismatic? Funny? Smart? The woman's interest will evolve over time as she gets to know him better. The man, on the other hand, is clearly interested, since he selected the woman based on her appearance (including fashion choices, hairstyle, the way she moves, etc.).

So, there is an imbalance in sexual attraction right from the beginning.

But that's not all. The disproportionate amount of attention placed on a woman's appearance and a man's personality means there is a discrepancy in what generates sexual arousal.

Our collective obsession with women's physical appearance results in the fetishization of the female body. Breasts. Ass. Mouth. Legs. Feet. Hair. Men's bodies are never worshipped in the same manner.

Because our culture places such focus on a woman's appearance, men receive much more visual sexual stimuli. On a first date, for example, the man's clothes are less likely to be as revealing or as colourful as the woman's. He won't be wearing makeup; his hairstyle will be simple. His date will not excessively fetishize his body, because she has not been conditioned to see it that way.

Simply realizing that they are prey, that they have no agency as hunters, stifles women's libido. What's the use of being attracted to a man if they can't make the first move? If they are expected to wait for something to happen, to see if they pique his interest? Under these circumstances, it makes much more sense to maximize their power of seduction and entice as many men as possible to approach them. Female desire thus becomes *secondary.*

The hunt arouses a man's excitement, since it forces him to consider his immediate desires — which are based on criteria that can be assessed in an instant. But the prey's arousal is less pressing. Women tend to defer their desire.

By having to wait passively, women are also made to follow the pace set by the man. Take a first date: If a woman feels the urge to kiss the man at 8:30 p.m. but waits for him to make the move (as per her role), by the time he actually does kiss her (let's say around 9:15 p.m.), the moment when she might have experienced the most pleasure may have passed. Similarly, a kiss that takes places at 7:45 p.m. might be too early for her. Whoever makes the first move always sets the pace.

I used the example of a kiss above, but the same notion applies to oral sex, penetration, or fondling. The woman must stay in her role as prey, even during sex. And regrettably, this leaves many women unsatisfied in bed.

Obviously, intercourse requires two people, and, barring some rare synergy (more a fantasy than a reality), one of them will have to initiate it; the other reacts. But the traditional dynamic between heterosexuals dictates that the man leads and the woman follows. There is little room for variation.

This hunter-hunted relationship has a further consequence when it comes to libido: the man also leads in terms of ideas for sexual activities, since he is the master of ceremonies. He conceives of an action, and he carries it out.

The hunter approach also prompts a sense of urgency. A man's adrenaline will surge the moment his prey appears responsive to his advances; he jumps at the chance, lest the woman change her mind and call things off. And the fear of not sealing the deal may make his desire surge faster than the woman's.

His prey — who has not hunted or sexualized him as he has done to her, and who is not motivated by the fear of missing an opportunity (she assumes the man is after sex at all costs) — will lag even further behind the man in terms of desire.

Women are expected to observe multiple contradictory imperatives while being pursued, which curb their desire and amplify their ambivalence. What strategy should they take when a man makes advances? Resist because they're interested? Resist because they're not interested? Not resist, and let things happen? None of these eliminate the fear of being reproached, taken for a sex maniac, or labelled a cocktease, and that goes a long way in subduing their desire.

Moreover, libido is closely linked to self-esteem. Someone with a strong sense of self-worth is in a better position to feel sexual excitement or desire for others. It follows that a woman who laughs at a man's jokes throughout courtship helps boost his libido and his self-esteem at the same time.

Of course, men also try to bolster the self-esteem of the women they want to seduce, for instance, by complimenting their appearance in order to please them. But praising a woman's appearance is a double-edged sword: it can also lead to a sense of insecurity when it comes to sex. Women are well aware that a naked body may not have the same allure as it does in a cute dress. "Does he still think I'm sexy when he can see *everything*? When I'm not wearing a bra? Can he see my love handles? How does my hair look? Is my mascara running?" Women have much to worry about, because they know the important role appearance plays during the courtship phase. Yet men don't feel less funny or less charismatic when they take off their clothes; such "skills" are simply no longer relevant. They therefore have fewer concerns during sex. While men also suffer from body image issues, they can rest easy knowing their power of seduction does not hinge primarily on their appearance. Their desire is not affected by these insecurities.

The way that our culture creates and fuels body image issues in women essentially places their self-esteem in the hands of men. When confronted with a woman seeking approval, a man has the immense power to reassure her, or to make her more vulnerable by withholding the long-awaited approval. The verdict may be encouraging or devastating; regardless, our culture, which consistently nurtures women's body image fears, fosters a dependency on men.

Indeed, if a woman doesn't already, it falls to her partner to "teach her to love her body" by lavishing compliments on it and admiring it for her. It is somewhat ironic that many of these complexes have been so deeply and irreversibly etched into women's minds that even when a man tries to reassure, he often fails.

Of course, men may also experience anxiety in the bedroom, but it is most often linked to sexual performance (achieving and maintaining an erection, making a woman orgasm, etc.). Which brings us back once again to their role as *active*

And while men fear the humiliation of a poor performance, the woman's passive role comes with different risks — which may even prove dangerous for her safety.

PASSIVENESS AND RAPE CULTURE

Since 2014, there has been much discussion on the topic of rape culture: the tendency in our culture to trivialize sexual assault.

Public conversation has largely focused on the consequences of rape culture for the victims of sexual assault (i.e., difficulty being believed and obtaining justice). But what still escapes notice is the unbalanced sexual dynamic that sets the stage for rape culture.

Whenever I'm asked in public to define rape culture, I say that it is what happens before, during, and after a sexual assault. *After*, when we vilify and ignore the victim. *During*, when the offender normalizes the abuse and delegitimizes the victim's experience. *Before*, when our ideas of sex eroticize sexual assault against women, or, quite simply, when women are objectified.

Women's passive role when it comes to sexuality is intrinsically linked to rape culture.

Feminists who criticize rape culture question the events that unfold after an assault; but few, I think, question the view of sexuality that imposes the role of prey onto women. Perhaps because it seems more urgent to help the victims and get justice for these women. But unless we attempt to challenge our traditional view of heterosexual sex and how it makes women vulnerable, the prevalence of this type of abuse is unlikely to diminish.

It is important to introduce and reinforce the notion of consent — but it isn't enough. We must also promote the idea of *reciprocity* in sexual relations so that women are no longer seen as receptacles of desire; we must stop normalizing their passivity. I want to show how the passive role imposed on women in a heterosexual relationship contributes to rape culture.

In the stereotypical game of seduction, a consenting woman gives subtle visual and vocal cues before engaging in sex. She might smile, run her hand through her hair, blush, or laugh at a joke. The signs of passive consent are not as clear as those of active consent (such as approaching, touching, or undressing a partner).

When we consider this kind of reserve to be the appropriate or "normal" sexual behaviour, we actively put women in danger. We place them in a grey area where everything is subject to interpretation, everything is ambiguous.

The notion that female desire is inherently passive means that to many people, if a woman does not explicitly say "no" to a man — or further, if she doesn't put up a fight when he takes control of her body — we can legitimately say that she consented. That she did not actively participate in the supposedly consensual act does not seem problematic.

Advocates of verbal consent try to free us from this trap. They argue that consent must be clearly stated, and that there's no such thing as implied consent. They maintain that "silence is not consent."

But again, this view places the person giving consent in the role of prey — or we might just as well say "a woman." It also places the man to whom she expresses her will in the role of predator. If we really hope to adhere to "silence is not consent," and since, legally, consent may be withdrawn at any time, the person leading the proceedings (the man) must continually ask during the encounter, "May I do this? May I keep doing it? What about this? May I do that, too?" And his prey must answer every question with "Yes. Yes. Yes." Which is why many well-meaning people are resistant to framing consent in this way. They find it infantilizing, and argue that it takes the fun and excitement out of the bedroom.

In fact, sexual partners give and withdraw consent for various actions every day, without it creating problems — even if they don't always verbalize it.

Let's assume that most men are capable of recognizing consent, through verbal cues or otherwise. Still, others may take advantage of the myth of women's innate sexual passivity to assault them. Aggressors view a woman's body as theirs for the taking, a receptacle for ejaculation, an assembly line of fantasies. A woman is a masturbatory doll.

These two ends of the spectrum can help us understand why heterosexual men tend to balk when it comes to talking about consent. Men know that since they initiate sex, it falls to them to secure consent. They are obliged to self-monitor. We therefore ask them to put a bit of fear behind their actions: they should be afraid of raping in order to avoid raping.

Conversely, few women are afraid of raping men. Then again, it's fairly easy not to violate a partner's consent when you're neither initiating nor directing sex.

Some women are also resistant to the notion of affirmative consent (the idea that a sexual act must begin with an explicit "yes"), because they enjoy seeing themselves as prey (often it is these women who defend street harassment) and they enjoy being pursued. They consent to having men not solicit their consent. It may seem paradoxical, but it is nonetheless conceivable once you buy into the notion of predatory seduction, precisely the model of seduction that excites us. This preference isn't inherently problematic: a woman who tells a man he can do "whatever he wants" is exercising her freedom. But clearly her personal desire should not be perceived by men as the universal preference among women.

The problem is not that one individual enjoys being pursued relentlessly. Rather, the problem is that we interpret this attitude as a preference that applies to all women. The problem is that being a woman means being predisposed to getting assaulted, because women are automatically seen as passive receptacles for male attention and advances. A person's gender has an impact on their likelihood to either suffer or commit assault.

It is difficult to foster empathy within a culture where sex is a unilateral activity between an active man and a passive woman.

Someone who is rarely put in a position of vulnerability, who does not consider themselves to be potential prey, will have a hard time taking the emotions of the other person into account. It's easier not to bother

"MAKE IT HURT, JOHNNY"
NOT "MAKE IT HURT, JOANIE"[10]

While anyone can have a taste for sex involving consensual and controlled humiliation or physical violence, custom dictates it is the woman who is most often the subject of these practices. Analysis of today's pornography proves this fact. According to a 2015 study on the fifty bestselling porn videos, 88 percent of verbal attacks and 94 percent of signs of physical violence were directed at women. These numbers have increased since the 1980s (78 percent and 73 percent, respectively).[11]

trying to understand why a partner is hesitating, when her role is thrust upon her automatically.

If we truly consider sex to be an equal partnership between individuals acting together, consent becomes imperative. Yet many still refuse to acknowledge that the hunter/prey dynamic is a tradition that needs dismantling, rather than a biological fact.

Our tendency to construe women as biologically passive comes up again and again when we study animal sexual behaviour. In his book *What Do Women Want?*, Daniel Bergner cites researcher Kim Wallen, who studied rhesus monkeys. Wallen describes how scientists in the 1970s were convinced that female rhesus monkeys are sexually passive, when they are, in fact, dominant.[12] When they want sex, the females pursue males to the point of harassment. It has since been observed that females play a highly active role among capuchin monkeys, Tonkean macaques, and pig-tailed macaques. Female orangutans and bonobos also display dominant behaviour.

Though there are always risks to comparing animal and human sexuality, it is a mistake to think all female primates are passive by default, and to then extrapolate that human nature is not so different.

2

Cougars and Nymphets:
Glorifying the Younger Woman

Men don't age better,
they're just allowed to age.
— Carrie Fisher

In 2014, fifty-three-year-old George Clooney married Amal Alamuddin, a lawyer in her midthirties. The day after the news broke, I sat with my coffee, reading a column by a journalist in her fifties who considered the relationship proof of a mid-life crisis, an ugly reality that can strike indiscriminately and leaves no aging wife safe in her marriage. As I came across similar stories, I couldn't help wondering whether the phenomenon is really as widespread as they say. I am, after all, about the same age as Amal Clooney. If the phenomenon is real, that means many women under thirty-five are dating men ten, fifteen, even twenty years their senior. So where are all the single men my age hiding?

Statistically speaking, there should be a single man out there for every single heterosexual woman — after all, the population is fairly evenly split between the genders.

If men in their fifties prefer to date younger women, then it follows that there are fewer younger women available. Logically, this should create an untapped pool of single young men who are potential partners for the older women. If this is the case, then why do we often hear about the former situation (older men with younger women) but rarely the latter (older women with younger men)?

Is the older man + younger woman combination really so common? And if the answer is yes, wouldn't it invariably lead to young men and older women coupling up?

Enter the "cougar": if we're talking about courtship, age gaps, and the hunt, we can't gloss over this contemporary female archetype.

Throughout history, women have been expected to abandon their sex drive as they aged, simply because it was believed that men lost interest in them. A woman was supposed to pass without protest from spring blossom to fading bloom.

Until recently, this shift manifested with motherhood. A woman would transition from eligible maiden, to bride, to mother. And once the kids arrived, the role of mother replaced that of sexual being and object of desire.[1] Women were expected to steer their lives according to this trajectory. First, devote body and soul to securing a husband; once this has been achieved, raise their children with the same utter devotion. A mother was not expected to attract men once she had settled down: her life had taken a new direction, one that desexualized her.

In today's world, with sexuality being trivialized and multinational corporations constantly hunting for new markets, the situation has changed. Mothers are no longer encouraged to renounce their sex appeal. On the contrary, marketing firms do everything they can to sell women products designed to keep them looking young. The imperative to appear youthful ensures that these products (hair dyes, push-up bras, makeup, anti-aging creams, plastic surgery, trendy clothing, etc.) are in constant demand.

This is partly why becoming a mother no longer stands in the way of a woman's sexualization. And this has given rise to two new cultural phenomena: the cougar and the MILF.

The MILF (Mother I'd Like to Fuck) and the cougar are two distinct concepts. A MILF is a woman who is objectified. A man's desire is central to the expression: the man is the subject, the "I," who is acting on the object. The sex drive of the mother in question is not part of the equation.

But while the MILF complies with the stereotype of the passive woman, the concept of the cougar is quite revolutionary.

The cougar is a subject who desires; her sex drive is central to the expression defining her. The image of the "cougar" suggests a predatory relationship. The cougar is no prey; she is a huntress.

But even so, does the cougar undermine the cumshot principle? This question deserves a closer look.

The cougar is no longer a spring blossom, but nor is she necessarily a mother. The word simply refers to a woman who is attracted to men significantly younger than she is.

The term entered popular culture around the turn of the millennium to describe celebrities like Demi Moore or Madonna. But New Zealand researchers Zoe Lawton and Paul Callister have traced the expression's origin to Canada, in the 1980s.[2] According to their research, the Vancouver Canucks, a professional hockey team, coined the term to refer to older single women who attended games in the hopes of sleeping with attractive young players. The expression was then picked up by columnist Valerie Gibson of the *Toronto Sun* in 2001. The following year, Gibson published a book providing tips for older women who want to date younger men. In it, she related her own experiences with men ten to twenty years her junior.

The age difference in Gibson's case is significant, but it isn't always so for cougars. A woman may be called a cougar even if she is only a few years older than her partner. In fact, the unusual nature of any relationship involving an older woman and a younger man is quickly remarked on — and amplified. Once, when I was twenty-nine and dating a twenty-five-year-old, an acquaintance compared our "age difference" to that of her own relationship: she was thirty, her partner fifty.

Yet in our culture, men can easily be older than their partner without raising any eyebrows. People may call attention to a large age gap, but not systematically and with less intensity. Why is that?

AGE DIFFERENCES IN FICTION

The older man/younger woman liaison is very common in fiction. Consider the famous Hollywood Age Gap, that all-too-common practice within the entertainment industry of pairing older male actors with much younger female partners.

Here are just a few examples:

- Jennifer Lawrence with Bradley Cooper in *Silver Linings Playbook* and in *Serena* (fifteen-year difference), and with Christian Bale in *American Hustle* (sixteen years);
- Emma Stone with Michael Keaton in *Birdman* (thirty-seven-year difference), with Joaquin Phoenix in *Irrational Man* (sixteen years), and with Colin Firth in *Magic in the Moonlight* (twenty-eight years);
- Scarlett Johansson with Bill Murray in *Lost in Translation* (she was eighteen and he was fifty-two — a thirty-four-year difference).

This is only a handful of examples among countless. Note that we don't call men in these movies "pumas" (a little-used term for men who pursue younger women[3]).

In 2015, Maggie Gyllenhaal made the shocking revelation in an interview that Hollywood had deemed her "too old" to play the love interest of a fifty-five-year-old man. She was thirty-seven at the time.

Today, the average age gap between on-screen partners is four and a half years (men are, of course, older).[4]

According to data gathered by the website GraphJoy, which charted age differences during the careers of twenty of Hollywood's top actors, male celebrities begin to be cast opposite much younger actresses once they reach thirty-five. While they age progressively onscreen, their romantic partners do not.[5]

ON THE TRAIL OF THE COUGAR

Now that we have a clearer picture of the phenomenon, it's worth exploring whether the "cougar" is more myth than reality.

Reuters, for one, has concluded that it is largely myth. In a release that was later picked up by various other media outlets, the news agency referenced a University of Wales Institute study from 2010, which discovered that despite embracing this new female figure in popular culture, women still prefer older partners and men continue to seek younger women.[6]

The study did not focus on the existence of the cougar, per se, but examined gender preferences internationally, across fourteen countries. It found that the cougar phenomenon is real, but relatively marginal. In fact, the study only confirmed what statistics already showed: we tend to form relationships in which the man is older than the woman.

Lawton and Callister, however, took a closer look at the cougar phenomenon. They observed that over a twenty-year period (1986–2006), the proportion of fifty-year-old women with a partner at least five years their junior jumped from 4 percent to 7 percent.

Interestingly, the proportion of fifty-year-old men in a relationship with a woman at least five years younger dropped from 35 percent to 31 percent over the same period.

These results were confirmed when the researchers compared their findings against statistics from the United States. Between 1960 and 2007, the proportion of marriages in which the man is at least five years older than his partner dropped from one-third to one-quarter. As for couples in which the woman is older, the percentage increased from 4 percent to 6 percent.

While these may be small fluctuations, the statistics do reflect real changes. Most age gaps still reflect a tendency to favour pumas, although the number of cougars has risen slightly.

The researchers noted, however, that their statistics describe only couples in long-term relationships; they did not look at dating or one-night stands, cases in which the cougar phenomenon is doubtless more prevalent.

The fact remains that the older woman/younger man model seems less natural to us. This is confirmed on dating sites like OkCupid, where women of all ages seek out men their age or older, while men over thirty continue to prefer women in their early twenties.[7]

Pornography offers a clear illustration of men's obsession with younger women. One of the most popular categories — if not *the* most popular, according to available data — is "teen" porn, where videos portray teen girls, not teen boys. In this case, *teen* really means *teen girls*. Actresses are required to be of legal age to perform on-screen, but they also are required to look young enough to pass for an adolescent. Just think of how the "sexy schoolgirl uniform" trope eroticizes teen girls.

How do we explain that one?

NYMPHET OBSESSION: A MATTER OF BIOLOGY?

All kinds of explanations grounded in biology have been used in the past to present this sexual preference as the natural order of things. Advocates have claimed that men are attracted to younger women due to "reproductive instincts." Because younger women are more fertile, they naturally are more sought after.

And since men remain fertile throughout most of their life, their age does not pose an issue for women from a reproductive standpoint. On the surface, it all seems to make sense.

But on closer inspection, this argument runs aground for a few reasons.

First, a progressive decline in women's sex appeal once they hit their midtwenties is not in our best reproductive interests. While fertility does begin to decline around this age, overlooking these women would mean losing out on innumerable chances for procreation.

Many women can conceive until they hit menopause, which occurs at fifty-one, on average. A *decline* in fertility does not mean that women over thirty become infertile overnight.

We tend to exaggerate the drop in women's fertility rates by implying the threat strikes early and hard. After reading numerous cautionary articles, I, too, long held the belief that when a woman reached her midtwenties, it was the beginning of the end. But according to a 2004 study, 82 percent of women between thirty-five and thirty-nine will get pregnant within a year of having regular sex. In another study, published in 2013, 78 percent of women in this age range conceived within the year, compared to 84 percent for women twenty to thirty-four years old. It appears, then, that the decline in fertility is not nearly as abrupt as many would have us believe. Women don't experience a significant drop in fertility until their forties, and even then a notable percentage are still able to conceive at that point.[8] Women who have not hit menopause are still very much within "child-bearing age."

Another argument focuses on the dangers associated with late child-bearing — and the risks are real. According to one UK study, the risk of Down syndrome climbs to one in eighty-five pregnancies for women over forty.[9] But is that number actually so high? Only if you look at it in terms of an optimal "natural" pregnancy.

To be fair, we must consider that scientists have also recognized the father's age as a risk factor for Down syndrome — one that contributes to anywhere from 11 to 50 percent of cases, studies show.[10] But the general public often fails to realize the risk related to the father's age.

There are also risks associated with adolescent births. According to the World Health Organization, "complications from pregnancy and childbirth are the leading cause of death among girls aged 15–19 years globally." From a reproductive standpoint, this is not advantageous. In addition, babies born to adolescent mothers are at greater risk of "having low birth weight with long-term potential side effects."[11] All this, and yet the fantasy of the teenage girl continues to burn brightly.

The chief logical flaw with the argument that men are biologically programmed to be attracted to very young women, however, lies elsewhere. Symbols of beauty and femininity that have appealed to men for many decades in the West signify extreme youth, and have nothing whatsoever to do with women's fertility — on the contrary.

Here are a few examples:

1. **Absence of pubic hair, leg hair, and underarm hair**
   Hair appears with the onset of puberty — a sign of approaching fertility — yet to be considered attractive, women are expected to remove this hair.

2. **A slender figure and narrow hips**
   Women's hips widen during puberty, but the overwhelming majority of actresses and models who embody sex appeal in our eyes have thin, narrow figures that are almost childlike.

3. **Blond hair**
   Among white people, blond hair is a sign of youth; it usually darkens to brown throughout adolescence or into adulthood. Although blond hair in adults is common in certain countries, the gene responsible for hair colour is not sex-linked. Despite this, the number of blond women in the street and on-screen vastly outweighs the number of blond men. Why? Women dye their hair, since blond hair

is particularly desirable — another indication of our preference for a childlike appearance.

1. Disproportionately large eyes

Large eyes are a common feature in children. As we age, our eyes stop growing well before the head, thereby reducing the head-to-eye proportion in adults. To increase their sex appeal, women apply mascara, fake eyelashes, eyeliner, and eyeshadow to make their eyes look bigger.

Small noses and full lips are other childlike features that are considered sexually desirable. Women often use makeup or plastic surgery to try to reproduce these features.

In the West, only a preference for full breasts breaks with this tendency. Barring that, it's clear that most physical attributes we consider to be sexy evoke childhood: i.e., a period when women are not yet fertile.

Pre-pubescence is considered highly attractive.

What we value in terms of sexual attractiveness, then, does not correspond with optimizing reproduction. As a result, we are forced, as a culture, to create a compromise: we demand that women of child-bearing age resemble infertile prepubescent girls to attract men.

This brings us to the archetype of the woman-child.

The fertility argument as an explanation of our collective attraction for young women weakens even more when we consider that *the signs proving a woman IS fertile are NOT seen as erotic.*

The "evolutionists" love drawing connections between women's physiques, their fertility, and men's preferences. Yet there are visible and unambiguous signs of fertility that these experts curiously overlook: traces of a past pregnancy. Stretch marks, sagging breasts, enlarged and darkened nipples, weight gain, and a soft belly are all signs a woman has already had a child and is therefore … *fertile*! A man who wants to reproduce with a woman who has never given birth is taking his chances — she may prove infertile — but a woman who has already had a child has undeniably demonstrated her capacity in this department.

So why is it that the signs of a previous pregnancy aren't considered the highest draw in terms of sex appeal? Why are they instead seen as embarrassing and ugly? We go so far as to expect mothers to erase all physical vestiges of pregnancy in order to appeal to men.

If women's fertility really had a decisive impact on men's libido, then society would value physical signs of previous pregnancies. But that's not the case.

For all these reasons, using fertility to explain men's "natural" attraction to younger women is a flawed argument. My point is not that fertility is irrelevant or that it isn't one variable in the equation. But I do believe it is not a sufficient explanation: it relies on too many paradoxes.

Now let's focus on women. Why do they prefer men their own age or older, regardless of how old they are?

We know that in theory, men, unlike women, can stay fertile their whole life. But the fertility of older men doesn't explain why they win out over younger men in terms of sexual attraction. Enter the explanation of man as provider during the Stone Age.

SPERM IS CHEAP

We tend to buy into different theories without considering their impact because we're drawn to ideas that validate our existing understanding of sexuality. In this respect, Bateman's principle offers a compelling argument. The theory essentially posits that because men produce millions of sperm with each ejaculation (in comparison to women, who produce just one egg per month), it isn't advantageous for them to limit their sexual attentions to one partner.[12] This explains why they have a natural tendency to womanize, to avoid checking their libido, while women tend to be more calculating when selecting potential partners before mating.

What this theory also (dubiously) implies is that men should have no reason to prefer any particular type of woman. It would be in their best interest to seize every opportunity to mate indiscriminately, with all sorts of women, to maximize their chances of reproduction. With no risk of getting pregnant, they have nothing to lose!

In other words: if a man's only goal is to procreate, then he should have no reason (biologically speaking) to be picky. Regardless of whether a woman is at the peak of her fertility or nearing the end of it, it's worth a shot if there's a possibility to reproduce.

Given this, responsibility for sex selection would not fall to philandering and indiscriminate men, but to fussier women.

Bateman's principle isn't watertight. However, note that while we love invoking the first part of the theory, which argues for men's sexual liberation and aims to free them from the "constraints" of monogamy, we tend to neglect the second part, which suggests that men should have no preferences for a woman's physique and age.

Here's how it goes: women are attracted to men who can provide for them. In prehistoric times, when we presume our ancestors were monogamous, women would have wanted a partner capable of supplying them and their future children with material resources. The division of labour dictated the man would go out in search of these resources while the woman took care of the children. There's no need to dwell on this model, which was the dominant ideology for centuries and still remains in currency to some extent. Given this context, however, a preference for an older man makes sense: older men were likely to have accumulated more resources. Partnering with an older man was advantageous because any future offspring would have a greater chance of survival.

However, the accumulation of goods and resources implies a structured, sedentary life that did not exist in primitive nomadic societies. This is an important distinction, since this model reflects a collective choice, a deliberate way of organizing society that is not rooted in any biological explanation. An attraction toward older men only makes sense rationally (from a reproductive standpoint) when the accumulation of resources becomes possible — and when it is men who accumulate them.

If we assume that women sought out monogamy during this "state of nature" or Stone Age, it would have been counterintuitive for them to reject younger men who were stronger and faster. Younger men had the best reflexes and were the most capable. They had better chances of bringing home fresh meat, ensuring the safety and comfort of the family, and fending off other males. In a primitive world, young men are the best providers.

Women, monogamous or not, will always have a vested interest in coupling with a powerful young man rather than an older one whose abilities are waning.

Today, women are artificially conditioned to set their sights on older men.

We rarely talk about it, but men are in their peak physical form between the ages of fifteen and twenty-five. Once they hit twenty-five, their abilities begin to decline.[13] By that logic, women should express a strong preference for men under twenty-five throughout their life. A man of thirty, forty, or fifty will never be as strong or resilient, his reflexes will never be as sharp, as a man in his twenties. The younger man is the more competent. He's the one who will be capable of bringing back the biggest mammoth for dinner.

From an evolutionary or biological perspective, there is no reason women should stop being "instinctively" attracted to young men as they age — which is the case we see with men.

We like to claim that men "age better" than women do, from a physical perspective. This idea is utterly absurd. Greying hair, baldness, wrinkles, and weight gain are all clear signs of aging that affect men and announce a decline in their physical prowess. Yet men don't seem to want to hide or mitigate them as much as women do.

Our cultural response to signs of aging in modern societies with an accumulation of resources differs drastically according to gender. These changes aren't necessarily considered negative when it comes to men. We associate older men with prestige, expertise, and credibility. In terms of sex appeal, a very concrete physical decline is compensated for by improved social status.

As we have already seen, popular belief holds that men don't experience fertility problems until late in life, and that a man's sperm quality declines somewhere around the age of sixty. But this is not true: the decline begins well before then, and it affects men's chances of reproduction. Men experience a gradual loss of testosterone beginning at around thirty. This hormone affects the production of quality sperm, as the urologist Harry Fisch explained to the *New York Times*.[14] Other researchers place this decline earlier, beginning in the early twenties.

On average, a twenty-five-year-old man will impregnate his partner after four and a half months of unprotected sex, while it takes men over forty nearly two years in similar conditions, according to researcher Karin Hammarberg.[15] The risk of miscarriage also doubles for men over forty-five.

And as I mentioned earlier, fetal health risks are also associated with fathers of advanced age, not just with mothers of advanced age.

Globally, a man's sexual abilities begin to drop off after age twenty: from then on, his sex drive will gradually decrease and the refractory period (recovery time needed between orgasms) will increase, until he eventually experiences erectile difficulties.[16] Even if men continue to produce sperm as they age, it loses potency and becomes more difficult to obtain.

Men, just like women, lose their sexual "relevance" from a reproductive standpoint as they age.

If men's clear preference for women under twenty-five were due to a biological predisposition to maximize their reproductive power, the same should go for women. A younger partner is more advantageous for them, too — on all fronts.

And so, the question remains: why do men show a marked preference for youth when it comes to sex, while on the whole women do not seem attracted to younger men? Why is the cougar phenomenon not more widespread in our culture? Why are childlike features (signs of pre-fertility) considered sexy in a woman? And why aren't signs of a past pregnancy considered sexy?

If our cultural biases encourage men to prefer youthful partners, it is in part because youth is a mark of submission. With maturity comes authority, and our patriarchal society promotes the idea of a heterosexual couple made up of a dominant male and a dominated female. The sexual roles during courtship and seduction described in the first chapter apply equally here: it's all part of the established order of things.

This observation leads me to a curious development in the rather overused archetype of the cougar.

As part of my work on TV,[17] I met with Valerie Gibson, the Canadian responsible for popularizing the term "cougar." During our interview, she acknowledged that while the concept initially referred to a mature woman in "hunting" mode, this is no longer the case. Gibson has observed a change in recent decades: today's young men are more likely to chase older women, who no longer need to actively seduce. Once again, women wind up being the prey.

What's more, "cougars" in relationships rarely correspond with our image of the rich and powerful woman. I also met with Milaine Alarie, a doctoral student at McGill University who is researching such couples. Her findings suggest that the wealthier a woman is, the less likely she is to date a younger man. Alarie also confirms what Gibson has observed: in couples where an age gap exists, it is frequently the younger men who chase the older women.

Given this reality, we have to ask ourselves: does the older woman/younger man model reflect a true revolution in the hunter/prey dynamic — or does it merely reproduce it?

Either way, a woman who is attracted to younger partners defies the classic heterosexual model. A cougar defies the status quo by refusing to sacrifice a desire for men at their physical and sexual peak, and refusing to submit to an older male. It isn't easy to break with sexual conventions; it's easier to say that only men are "naturally" attracted to youth.

Our culture, which legally infantilized women by placing them under the tutelage of men for centuries, continues to support a similar but informal guardianship, through the authority granted by age in heterosexual couples.

We like to think that love has no age — that it is blind. But the fact remains that these trends are observable, and that age generally comes with more financial stability, greater prestige, and a broader grasp of knowledge and culture. All these confer power to the older party in a social interaction. And when tradition

dictates that men are always the older person in the relationship, a pretty clear pattern emerges.

But that isn't all. There is another reason why men
— and often women — find the idea of a very young
woman intensely attractive. And that brings us to examine another effect of the cumshot principle.

3

The Purity Imperative:
Innocence — the Essence of the Slut

> "How will this be," Mary asked the
> angel, "since I am a virgin?"
> The angel replied, "The Holy Spirit
> will come upon you."
>
> — Luke 1:26–38

The archetype of the woman-child holds a powerful sex appeal: youth denotes purity, and purity is irresistible when the goal is transgression. As with other societies where patriarchal religions have infused sex with guilt for centuries, our Judeo-Christian culture directly associates sex with transgression. You could even say that to us, sex *is* transgression.

But what exactly is being transgressed? In a word: woman.

The cumshot principle holds that being a target is not enough: a woman must also be pure, so that it is exciting to sully her. Our notions of sex revolve around the idea that a woman is inherently unspoiled, naive, and virtuous — and that a man has the power to corrupt her with sex.

We are obsessed with the idea of dirtying that which is pure. The cliché of the woman begging to be defiled serves as an arousing sexual fantasy for many. This explains in large part why our culture fixates on a woman's youth. The younger the woman, the purer — and more corruptible — she is, and the more erotic we find her.

But purity isn't enough. Our dominant fantasy is actually more elaborate: the young woman, who starts off innocent, must end up being consumed by lust. That is the ideal outcome.

This is the tipping point we seek: we like to contrast the image of the sweet, innocent woman with that of the woman corrupted by sex.

"Come on, you whore, say you like it! I know you like it!" Injunctions like these, common in the porn industry (and in the bedroom), illustrate how central women's purity is to our sexuality. Ordering a woman to express her enjoyment of the sexual experience implies it isn't a given. We assume that either she has not been enjoying herself or she has remained silent in keeping with her role (real, presumed, or imaginary) of pure woman, detached from sex. And now, we want her to verbalize that she is giving herself up to the sex that is defiling her. The tension within the idea of a woman who at first doesn't accept her own enjoyment, then finally gives in and concedes, "I love it;

I'm a slut," is electrifying for the man ordering her to admit it. It may also be electrifying for the woman receiving the order, who is engaged in the same fantasy.

An incredible amount of porn revolves around a man corrupting a woman. Basically, we don't want a woman to want sex, until she does.

This model of sex is obviously harmful in its commentary on women's consent. It implies that consent is not given at the outset — even if, in reality, situations like these are part of a game, with consent given beforehand.

But even in the context of a game, the takeaway is that the woman must articulate she is enjoying what is being done to her — and by doing so she becomes a slut.

Take the term itself: *slut*. A slut is defined as "a woman who has many casual sexual partners." Synonyms include *tramp*, *whore*, *prostitute*, and *floozy*. By default, then, it is an adjective only used to describe women.

In French, the male form of the word *slut* effectively translates into the term *bastard,* which connotes a completely different field of meaning: "an unpleasant or despicable man, one who is disloyal or dishonest." Synonyms include *scoundrel* and *villain*. The word is pejorative, but it is free of sexual connotations. A bastard is someone who exhibits bad behaviour. A slut is a woman who exhibits bad behaviour *in relation to sex.*

We can, and do, use the adjective "slutty" to describe a man, but it often serves to reinforce his masculinity or his virility. A slutty man uses his arsenal of male weapons to sleep with as many women as possible. A slutty man is often congratulated, not disgraced.

Why the difference?

Our language doesn't give many tools to shame a heterosexual male for his libido or for how he exposes his body in public. There is literally no word to describe disgraceful sexual behaviour for a straight man. The notion only applies to women; the expression was invented for them.

The reason? The purity imperative only applies to women.

Sexual clichés for women focus on inexperience, youth, propriety, modesty, reserve, and naïveté — all qualities that evoke purity. But — crucially — our expectations don't end there. The same women also have to be "real sluts." A woman's purity must coexist with her sexual desire. Men don't truly want women to be pure, and women aren't actually pure. But our collective sex drive, conditioned by our Judeo-Christian and patriarchal heritage, feeds on the tension between the whore's eager "yes" and the good girl's modest "no" in the face of sex.

Purity is the determining characteristic of a slut. A woman can't become a slut if, fundamentally, she cannot be corrupted. A person who retains their dignity while expressing a sexual desire is not a slut. That's why men's purity isn't compromised during sex: no one expects them to be chaste to begin with. Expressing desire cannot debase their image.

Women are expected to be naughty. To throw seductive glances over their shoulders and blush. To wear sexy clothes without revealing too much. They must protect their virtue, but also crave the penis. They may be provocative at times, as long as they retain an air of purity, as long as their appearance or basic attitude continues to evoke innocence, youth, and submission.

We want women to be pretty, young, and naive — or, sweet and maternal — because these qualities are intrinsically linked to purity. We claim that these qualities protect women from men's debauchery. But in reality, the inverse is true: this feminine image fuels our erotic fantasies.

As a result, the pressure on women is twofold: they must evoke innocence while arousing sexual desire. In this way, the purity imperative imprisons women and their libido to a strange paradox.

PURITY PROPAGANDA

The purity imperative means fantasizing about the adolescent; the schoolgirl; the virgin. It's Lolita. It's Anastasia Steele in *Fifty Shades of Grey*. It's Marilyn Monroe. It's Paola in *La Dolce Vita*. It's Betty Boop. It's the MILF, with her maternal aura. It is the pedophilic fantasy.

There is no doubt that the purity imperative is rooted in religion. But male chauvinism is a separate factor behind this deeply sexist principle that guides women's socialization. As we have seen, the purity imperative establishes a code of conduct specific to women: "Stay young, stay naive; do not express your sexual desires, and do not sexualize men you are attracted to; most of all, be modest, do not be vulgar, and do not reveal your bodies excessively." When women do not conform to this code, they are no longer pure, and the possibility of corrupting them vanishes. Women must adhere to the purity imperative at all costs, in order to keep the fantasy of transgression alive.

And that is why we invented *slut-shaming*. The practice is a call to order aimed at one or several women, meant to instill a sense of guilt for behaviour or physical appearance when we judge that they have exceeded the limits of decency.

Slut-shaming is a judgment that is defamatory, patronizing, and insulting toward women, and downright reprehensible. It is a form of stigmatization that usually comes from someone who subscribes avidly to the purity imperative.

It is also, clearly, a social construction. Humans are not born with body issues; babies and children don't give a second thought to their physical appearance or their nudity. They don't have complexes; they don't feel shame. Kids running around naked are likely to laugh if you try to wrestle them into clothing. Loathing for the body doesn't happen until later.

All it takes is one person, in one moment, to change our perception of our body. From the moment the disease of modesty is introduced, our body goes from neutral material to impure. And when the transformation is over, we end up wanting to convince others that their bodies are offensive, too — especially those of women.

When we talk about slut-shaming, we often think of women bullying each other — one woman judging another based on sexual conduct or appearance. But according to statistics from the British think tank Demos, which analyzed thousands of tweets containing the words *slut* or *whore*, men engage in shaming as much as women do.[1]

Men and women have different motivations for verbally abusing women, even if they are all ultimately related to social control and the purity imperative. I will group these motivations into three categories: elitism, jealousy, and sexual conservatism.

Elitism

Slut-shaming is often used to establish the superiority of the social elite over women of lower classes.

Sociologists from the University of Michigan[2] studied female students who began university in 2004. They observed that women from wealthy families used "slut" to refer to peers from lower-income backgrounds in order to distance themselves from the latter, by criticizing their clothing or attitudes.

This study was concerned with young women stigmatizing each other, but men are also capable of elitism-motivated slut-shaming. A man might brag that he prefers women whose style is "classy" and not "trashy," without realizing that these distinctions reflect the fashion values of the elite; conveniently, the elite determine what is considered erotic and noble or indecent and crude. The elite establishes what good taste looks like.

Jealousy

Both genders can participate in slut-shaming motivated by hostility toward a particular woman.

For example, a woman who does not want to dress provocatively or engage in certain sexual behaviours might feel jealous of another woman who does so and reaps the rewards (i.e., attention).

Male resentment can also produce this sexist phenomenon. Men who lack a sex life may stigmatize women who have relations with other men. The hypothesis was first introduced by the University of Pennsylvania's Derek Kreager as part of a study that followed 921 students aged eleven to sixteen over five years.[3]

Sexual conservatism

Slut-shaming is ultimately a form of sexual conservatism — and this is the crux of the problem. It's symptomatic of a fear of change; many people are afraid of a paradigm shift when it comes to sex. They fear their fantasies will cease to excite them, that they'll be replaced by something else.[4] If this were to happen, the fundamental values around which their lives are organized would become obsolete. This would upend their lives and cause them to lose their meaning.

For instance, a woman who has always believed in the importance of remaining a virgin until marriage may be upset to learn her daughter is sexually active. Similarly, a woman who has never worn leggings outside of a gym may be offended to see other women wearing them in public.

When we organize our lives around a central principle and believe ourselves to be moral by adhering to it, we are shocked to learn that for others it may hold no value whatsoever. If others flaunt the rule, then why have we been holding back all these years? It's mind-boggling.

Each generation is appalled by the behaviour of subsequent generations, particularly when it's a question of sex. Each generation believes it has finally reached the "right" level of sexual liberation. We all think our parents were too uptight, and fret that our children go too far.

Sexual conservatism in men may also be prompted by the fear of impotence. I observe this phenomenon every time I talk about the need to desexualize breasts. In our culture, women's breasts — whose biological function is to feed babies — are considered sexy and erotic. We force women to hide them, while men are entitled to display theirs. Male and female breasts are made up of the same tissue, only men's are typically smaller. Censoring the chest of one and not the other is a sexist societal choice (there have been many societies throughout history that did not choose to do so). I write extensively about the discrimination against women's bodies and, without fail, a number of male readers are astonished to discover that breasts can be desexualized. They are scared that the female chest will become mundane and lose its sex appeal for them.

They therefore insist that women should be prohibited from baring their chest in public. Men's collective fear of no longer being excited by breasts leads to the injunction that women should not consider this part of their body as "normal." Women's breasts must retain their sexual mystique, which can only be accessed in the bedroom or by watching porn.

And many heterosexual women feel the same way. Their breasts represent a sexual asset; women fear that their powers of seduction would be diminished if baring their breasts in public were to become socially acceptable.

PROHIBITING WOMEN'S BODIES

Our relationship with women's breasts is a good example of how we prohibit that which we eroticize. For
those turned on by the fantasy of sexual purity, women's
bodies must remain hidden. It goes a little like this:

We consider something to be sexual, so we censure
it ⟩ we censure it, thereby creating sexual tension around
it ⟩ we feel sexual tension in relation to the thing, leading us to consider it sexual ⟩ we see it as sexual, so we
censure it. Wash, rinse, repeat.

There's no escaping it: to censure = to eroticize. It's a
truly vicious cycle.

Let's consider dress codes for female high-school
students. Teenagers who make headlines by contesting
these rules (by refusing to wear a bra or by challenging
authority when a skirt is judged too short) exemplify
this dynamic.

It's a paradox: we impose a dress code on students
who are supposedly overexposing themselves, and by
doing so we sexualize them. A prohibitive dress code is essentially an eroticizing process that creates sexual tension.

For years we have been hearing male teachers
complain that what their female students wear is "dis-
tracting." Instead of encouraging these men to do some
deeper reflecting, schools continue to hire teachers
who can't help sexualizing the young women they interact with; schools validate the teachers' behaviour by
requiring girls to cover their bodies so that they won't
"bother" the males (teachers and students alike) around
them. Twice I have been on the receiving end of these

judgments: reprimanded once by a primary-school teacher, and once by a high-school principal. I can still remember my shame and incomprehension. In my eyes, my clothes weren't scandalous. They were pretty, trendy outfits, and I felt comfortable wearing them. But in the eyes of the administration, they were an outrage, and by wearing them I had become a "situation."

School administrations contribute to female eroticization by laying out, in black and white, which parts of their bodies girls must hide. In their defence, one could argue that society already perceives these girls as erotic. And it's true. But even though the prevailing sexist culture sexualized the adolescent before and more intensely than schools did, they both subscribe to the same logic.

Schools argue that their dress codes apply to boys and girls equally, but this isn't entirely true — or rather, it isn't really relevant. Fashion trends differ by gender; therefore, no dress code penalizes girls and boys in the same way.

Many of these dress codes stipulate that girls' bra straps must not be visible. This creates a problem that only applies to girls. Nor do boys wear skirts at school (in fact, this would generally be prohibited). We might be tempted to argue that length of shorts could be a gender-neutral issue; but again, short-shorts are a uniquely female fashion trend. So, a boy can wear clothes that conform to the rules and still be fashionable. A girl who wears modest clothes that conform to the rules won't be. The social cost is not the same: girls and boys don't face the same dilemma.

Women's fashion, which rests on the cumshot principle, is focused on pushing the limits of what is considered decent and indecent. If girls are forced to hide parts of their bodies, playing with the parameters of this injunction can become a game.

Furthermore, our culture encourages girls to project an image of sexual availability. Some men even criticize slut-shaming to encourage girls to show more skin. "Girls who expose themselves are just affirming their sexuality, so leave them alone," goes the argument. While their discourse may appear noble, the underlying message is an essential part of the transgression equation. You must show yourself off so men find you attractive; you must reveal your body to be considered sexually interesting. By claiming that a girl who shows skin is just affirming her sexuality, we really mean that she is developing her sexuality by interiorizing the male gaze (and not by developing her own sexual perspective on others). It's all deeply hypocritical.

Teenage girls experience slut-shaming more than any other group. Our social institutions try to impose the purity imperative upon them above all, because the dominant fantasy centres on the image of the girl. This leaves teenage girls between a rock and a hard place.

On the one hand, they are expected to be modest, prudent, sweet, elegant, conscientious, and kind. We tell them to wait for love before losing their virginity. We want their sexual experiences to involve love, and we want them to take it very seriously. On the other hand, adults are constantly consuming their bodies through porn and in daily life. It's easy to picture a man publicly criticizing the so-called transgressions of a young pop singer or actress, then later watching teen porn in the privacy of his own home.

We bombard teenage girls with contradictory messages that require them to show off their bodies even while they hide them. To be pure and impure at the same time. Together, these demands generate a sexual tension that damages young girls and takes their psyches hostage.

The moment we take a position that reflects anything other than indifference, we can no longer claim neutrality in this ideological battle. By telling girls to either hide their bodies or to flaunt them, we help perpetuate the paradigm of transgression. The two demands, though apparently conflicting, work in tandem to construct this fantasy.

HYPERAWARENESS OF THE BODY

Our duplicity doesn't just apply to teenage girls; we begin to indoctrinate girls when they are quite young and easily influenced, to ensure they conform to the purity requirement *and* grow up to be potential sluts. These twisted expectations have lasting impacts on their sexuality.

First, they cause women to be hyperaware of their bodies. Women are constantly being asked to push limits but to never to exceed them. As a result, they become image experts who are obsessed with appearances. Knowing that the male gaze is constantly trained on them means that unlike men, women cannot take a casual attitude toward their appearance. Judgment and contempt are never far off — and neither are salacious looks.

At the same time, a young woman can never completely reject the idea of using her body. If she doesn't play the seduction game, she won't be considered feminine, and she will be judged accordingly. She might get called "ugly," "butch," "dirty," "square," or any number of other insults. We tell girls who reject female eroticization that they should "make more of an effort."

Being acutely and constantly aware of their appearance predisposes women to develop body image issues. And this can create significant hurdles in the bedroom.

This hyperawareness of the body, of its ability to arouse excitement while walking the thin line of "respectable femininity," prevents women from truly letting go, in a broad sense. Having a body that attracts an inordinate amount of attention does not create an easy route to sexual fulfillment.

The purity imperative is so deeply rooted that, for many women, giving themselves up to desire (the ultimate goal, according to the cumshot principle) becomes impossible.

I recently interviewed a woman who told me that when she has sex, it's as though there is an imaginary camera above her bed, filming her. She watches herself via this camera and doesn't like what she sees. It effectively kills the mood.

She's not the only one. Various sexologists have told me that women can become disconnected quite easily during sex. They have a harder time than men remaining present in the moment.

It's easy to tell women who struggle with these issues to simply "let go." Yet nothing could be less simple. In reality, women who strive to break free of the purity imperative must undo years and years of conditioning. Being told to let go won't help them erase everything the prevailing culture has been feeding them since birth. It's like the battle of David and Goliath.

Women's autonomy is undermined by the fantasy of purity that requires women to exercise restraint when it comes to sex. They're supposed to resist sex — not to seek it out whenever or however they want it.

This frequently leaves women unable to articulate what they want, having internalized that men lead the charge when it comes to sex. And it doesn't help that they grow up in a world that offers very little in the way of female-specific fantasies. Our culture does not provide women with fictional scenarios where men are the ones being transgressed. Women can't fuel their libido with fantasies that simply don't exist.

Thus, by default, women adopt fantasies created by men, for men. And they are thereby given a role: that of the pure maiden who transforms into a slut upon contact with a penis.

The purity imperative and the passive role imposed on women in the seduction dynamic function in complementary ways and have similar effects.

The purity imperative has women believe that deriving pleasure from sex should not be the end goal. Enjoyment is a fringe benefit that only happens when yielding to a man — whose own pleasure is the primary goal.

The woman's job, then, is to place a man's sexual pleasure at the centre of her own. This is the appropriate and dignified thing to do. By simply giving in to a man's desire, the modest and passive woman who climaxes the moment a man touches her has merely lost control. She is not responsible for her own pleasure or desire, and therefore remains "pure" for her next sexual encounter. Her honour is safe.

4

Sex Segregation:
From Objectification to Autophilia

> I can't concentrate in flats.
> — Victoria Beckham

Our relationship with the female body is a melodramatic one.

Our obsession with female anatomy compels women both to conceal and to exhibit their bodies. A woman must expose her body — in part, only, but without a doubt. From a visual standpoint, that's what femininity means to us: flirting with the limits of the decent and indecent.

Let's take a closer look.

Our society has countless unwritten rules separating women from men. This sex segregation has become a well-oiled system that we treasure. We are, on the whole, allergic to questioning the status quo.

Historically, we have physically separated men and women, segregating the spaces in which they evolve. We created schools for girls and schools for boys, assigned men to public spaces while confining women to the home, and established traditionally feminine or masculine professions. Consider pilots and flight attendants: literally separated by a physical barrier.

Today we continue to separate men and women, in public restrooms and locker rooms, when we play sports or when we dance, on official forms (by checking *Ms.* or *Mr.*, *F* or *M*), in language (through the use of gendered pronouns), in toy stores, and in clothing stores. This final example holds particular interest for me, because it illustrates how we differentiate our bodies *visually*, which impacts our libidos in certain ways.

WHEN EYES REPLACED NOSES

For most members of the animal kingdom, pheromones are what stimulate libido. These chemical signals transmit information between members of a species and trigger a sexual attraction. Humans also secrete pheromones, but we have lost the capacity to detect them: the vomeronasal organ, located in the nose, has atrophied. In its place, culture has taken over for nature, and we have collectively constructed our sex drive around our sense of sight.

We therefore create symbols, continuously and deliberately, that we associate with courtship and sex. These symbols are visual stimuli.

It seems that we aren't satisfied with merely temporarily segregating based on gender for specific activities — swing dancing, for instance, or urinating. Far from it. We want to be able to know, with just a glance and even from a distance, whether the silhouette on the horizon belongs to a man or a woman. Regardless of the age or size of the person in question, we are determined that the genders should appear fundamentally distinct the moment we register them. To do this, however, we can't rely only on anatomical differences: we need more. Men and women must be symbolically opposed.

In the Bible, sex segregation through clothing is ordained by God: "A woman shall not wear a man's garment, nor shall a man put on a woman's cloak, for whoever does these things is an abomination to the Lord your God."[1]

Male and female fashion is designed to achieve this differentiation.

This is another direct consequence of the cumshot principle. As we have already seen, women must be passive targets to receive a man's desire. A woman must embody purity so men will want to defile her. But she must also be easily identifiable so we can know at a glance that she (unlike a man) is above all a body to examine, criticize, or admire.

As I write these lines, sitting outside a downtown café of a major Western city, I watch the passersby who are out enjoying the glorious weather. All are dressed according to their gender. Everything is differentiated: their hair, hats, shoes, shirts, the list goes on and on. Some are wearing accessories that could be considered androgynous — sneakers, for example — but when I take in the full picture, I notice certain characteristics that immediately identify them as men or women.

DEFINING FEATURES OF MALE AND FEMALE FASHION

Colour of clothing

Women's clothing is much more colourful: it is both brighter and more varied. Men generally wear dark or neutral colours such as grey, dark blue, brown, or black. Women's clothing also tends to include patterns and textures (flowers, polka dots, lace, etc.), which rarely feature in men's wardrobes.

Exposed skin

Clothing designed for men covers a greater surface area than clothing for women. Men's shorts and sleeves are longer (long sleeves cover the entire arm to the wrist, short sleeves cover the shoulder and upper arm). Collars almost always go as high as the neck.

Low-cut tops for women expose the neck, the area around the collarbone, and the top of the chest. Plunging necklines often reveal the top of the breasts, along with a woman's cleavage. Sleeves come in various lengths: full, three-quarter, short, sleeveless, spaghetti straps, or strapless. Depending on current fashion trends, tops may reveal the lower abdomen or a larger part of the belly (crop tops or belly shirts).

Women's shorts are also significantly shorter. While men's shorts are often cut just above the knee, women's shorts are cut at the mid-thigh, upper thigh, or even reveal the gluteal fold (where the buttocks meets the thigh).

Similarly, women's bathing suits expose more skin (although they stop at revealing the nipple, which is considered obscene).

Skirts and dresses

Worn almost uniquely by women in our culture, skirts and dresses are an unequivocal visual cue symbolizing the pinnacle of femininity. Until recently, this was actually the only attire permitted to women. Pants were not acceptable — in the same way that it is socially taboo for a man to wear skirts and dresses — until the twentieth century.

What's remarkable about these types of garments is how effectively they accomplish their role of creating sexual tension around the body. By definition, skirts and dresses are completely open at the bottom. Since they are not closed between the legs, a strong breeze or a deep bend at the waist and — oops! — it is possible to glimpse what should be kept hidden. This happens only rarely, but there is always a risk, nonetheless — which is what makes skirts and dresses so attractive, so feminine. Women who wear them must make sure to be well covered, to cross their legs while seated, to hold the skirt down in the wind, to check that their dress hasn't gotten caught in their underwear after a trip to the bathroom. And this hyperawareness of the body, this concern for maintaining a respectable appearance while simultaneously establishing conditions to prevent it, is the essence of femininity as we know it.

Tight clothing

When we think of a form-fitting garment, we immediately picture a little black dress clinging to the body, Bond-girl style. But beyond this cliché, the truth is that women's wardrobes largely consist of tight-fitting clothing.

Women's clothing is made to hug the body's curves, since we believe a woman's figure should be perceptible — in contrast to men's clothing, which is much looser-fitting. Men's pants are baggier, their T-shirts roomier, even their pullovers have a more spacious fit.

When men are required to dress up, they wear straight pants and a jacket or blazer over a button-up: a combination that conceals their figure. Women, meanwhile, wear form-fitting dresses that hug their every curve. And if the skirt is loose or long, the bodice will be even more revealing.

Of course, women also have more relaxed clothing in their closets; but these items are paired with fitted pieces to create a hide-and-seek effect with the silhouette, according to the fashion trends of the day. And when an outfit is skin-tight, it leaves nothing to the imagination. These clothes are unforgiving; we can see every roll, every bulge.

Since this type of clothing is so uncompromising, women whose bodies don't conform to our beauty standards develop strategies to hide their "flaws." For instance, they might wear control-top undergarments that suck in their hips or waist — essentially a modern-day corset. Older or plumper women might also wear loose-fitting clothing with lots of layers for a "deceiving" effect that helps them hide their bodies. In doing so, they stray from the feminine ideal, which dictates that women display their figures. But they are forgiven — and even encouraged — since we believe "imperfect" women shouldn't be sending visual stimuli when it comes to sex, anyway.

For women who aspire to femininity despite their imperfections (i.e., the majority of women), there are all sorts of highly sophisticated ways to exhibit and camouflage. We've all seen the magazine articles and fashion blogs offering readers a how-to guide to dressing for your figure: *You* have a pear-shaped body. *You're* an inverted triangle. These teach women to use clothing to conform to society's collective beauty ideals.

Tight clothing can be remarkably ruthless, and in this respect the G-string or thong has proved a particularly effective invention. This tiny piece of fabric has a narrow strip that passes between the buttocks so as not to cover the cheeks. It was popularized when fitted pants came into style, and is intended to erase all visible traces of undergarments on this eroticized area of the body. The G-string was marketed to allow women to wear pants, shorts, dresses, or skirts that show off the shape of their buttocks without the view being disturbed by an underwear line — which might break the mysterious spell of femininity.

The same goes for pockets. Most of women's clothing has no pockets at all (including tiny or fake pockets), while pockets on men's clothes are perfectly functional. That's because pockets have a practical function, not just an aesthetic one, and when filled with objects can disrupt the linearity of a garment designed to hug a woman's curves. "Men have pockets to keep things in, women for decoration," Christian Dior famously said in 1954.

And don't forget that almost all women's pants shown in stores hug the buttocks — so consistently, in fact, that the expression "boyfriend jeans" was coined to refer to pants that do not. As the name indicates, only men (in theory) are expected to wear loose-fitting jeans; a woman who wears them most likely borrowed them from her boyfriend.

Cinching the figure

As we saw earlier, not all women's clothing is form-fitting. But when a garment is loose or baggy, women employ other strategies to feminize the outfit, such as adding a belt. A dress can be fitted with a sash or elastic sewn into the fabric to pull it taut in strategic areas, such as below the bust or around the waist: a visual reminder of the body concealed beneath the loose fabric.

Bras are another example of this phenomenon. Women in most societies throughout history did not wear bras. While many say they appreciate the comfort bras afford, bras are first and foremost a fashion accessory that cause *discomfort* for many women.

For decades, bras were marketed as a way to keep breasts from sagging prematurely. Yet there is no evidence to support this claim. According to Jean-Denis Rouillon, professor at the Centre hospitalier régional universitaire de Besançon who led a fifteen-year study of 130 women aged eighteen to thirty-five, bras actually contribute to sagging breasts.[2]

Although there is no evidence that wearing a bra helps combat the tendency of breasts to sag due to pregnancy, weight change, genetics, aging, and other natural causes, countless professionals still claim that bras provide the key to preserving firm breasts.

But if this supposed benefit is the goal, bras have a curious design: they lift the breasts and bring them closer together to enhance cleavage. How is this supposed to provide better support? Why reposition the breasts? And isn't there a risk of back pain by shifting women's centre of gravity?

Bras have an additional effect: they standardize the way breasts look and hide the nipple. From a glance, one would think women's breasts are all uniform, while in reality chests vary greatly. Bras are solid; they are modern corsets. Sitting breastless on lingerie store shelves, they proudly maintain their supports. Padding adds volume and hides the undignified nipple, and the underwire and overall stiffness illustrate how the bra is intended to change the chest's natural appearance. A woman must hide the true shape of her breasts or be considered unattractive — even offensive.

Shoes

Women's shoes are often designed without taking into account the foot's actual shape. That means women must develop skills to wear them. High heels are the best example: since they alter the foot's arch and overall position, these shoes are difficult to walk in, and downright dangerous where running is involved. They force women to take small, careful steps to avoid falling. Just wearing them can be painful.

Yet flat shoes can also pose a challenge. To keep ballet flats on the feet, for instance, a woman must contract her toes at each step. And since these shoes typically have very thin soles — a feature not generally found in men's footwear — they wear out quickly.

Whether heels or flats, women's shoes seem to have been designed primarily as decoration, and not to help the wearer get around more efficiently.

Hair and makeup: sexualizing the head

When we talk about our "relationship with our body," we don't always include the hair and face. But these features are also sexualized.

Makeup is nothing more than a sexualizing process to make the face appear more desirable. Lipstick accentuates lip colour, eyeliner appears to widen the eyes, mascara lengthens and emphasizes the eyelashes, foundation evens skin tone, blush highlights the cheekbones, eyeshadow makes eyes look bigger. In recent years, the Kardashian sisters have popularized the practice of contouring: using makeup and visual effects to radically change the face's appearance. Some are outraged by the practice, but the truth is that the sole purpose of all makeup, in contouring or otherwise, is to make the face as attractive as possible according to current trends.

Makeup is to the face what skirts and dresses are to the body: reserved only for women, the restriction itself a mark of femininity. Long hair, skirts, lipstick: the more a practice is exclusive to women, the more those who adhere to it are considered feminine.

And what about hair? One might argue that men, too, can wear their hair long. While this is true, long hair is generally considered a feminine feature, and it tends to be discouraged for men.

Standard practice dictates that women wear their hair long (chin-length, shoulder-length, or all the way down the back) and men wear their hair short (shaved, or two to five centimetres long). Fashion trends allow for variations, but we invariably return to the "men = short hair/women = long hair" binary.[3]

Men's hairstyles are practical. Short hair doesn't get windblown or fall across the eyes. Conversely, many hairstyles for women — even short ones — are designed to obstruct vision and require constant upkeep and attention. Long hair limits the peripheral vision when it's not pulled back. A woman can be nearly blinded by her own hair if she bends over. Long hair gets tangled easily and requires brushing. But that isn't all. We expect women to care for their hair using products, such as hair dryers, straighteners, curling irons, hairspray, mousse, special shampoo, extensions, barrettes, elastics, and bobby pins, to name just a few.

A woman's daily hair maintenance requires a significant time investment.

As a woman working in the television industry, I see first-hand how much time it takes women to care for their face and hair. CBC schedules approximately forty-five minutes of prep time before female journalists and news anchors go on the air, compared to about five to ten minutes for their male colleagues. In other words: the national television network in Canada thinks a woman needs thirty-five to forty extra minutes of prep time just to appear as presentable as a man. Is a woman's natural state really so offensive?

Hair care doesn't end with daily maintenance. A large number of women dye their hair, as well. As women age, they tend to colour their hair to cover the grey, while men are more likely to embrace theirs ("silver foxes" like George Clooney are even considered sexy). Even younger women dye their hair if they feel their natural colour isn't vibrant or blond enough, or simply to conform to current trends. Here we come back to the notion that colour denotes femininity. As with clothing, women's hair is expected to be more colourful, and therefore more visible.

Body hair

Managing body hair is a particularly sex-differentiated practice. Men trim their beards, but in most cases that is the extent of their hair care. Yet for decades, women have been expected to shave their legs, under their arms, between their thighs — not to mention removing any stray hairs on their faces.

Plastic surgery

When we talk about the importance both genders place upon appearance, it has become fashionable to claim that men are, in fact, "catching up" to women. We argue that men today are just as preoccupied by their looks as women are, and just as likely to make alterations in order to please. This is a prevalent discourse when it comes to plastic surgery, but the figures tell a different story.

According to statistics published by the International Society of Aesthetic Plastic Surgery, women accounted for 86 percent of all plastic surgery patients in 2014. This number doesn't even come close to 50 percent parity.

What's more, a 2015 publication by the American Society of Plastic Surgeons reports that 92 percent of so-called minimally invasive surgeries were performed on women, compared to 8 percent on men. The numbers for conventional plastic surgery indicate a ratio of 87 percent female and 13 percent male. And while there has been an increase in both types of surgeries over the long term, the rise has been more significant in women (+118 percent) than men (+24 percent).[4] These statistics contradict the idea that men are "catching up" to women in this department.

THE BODY, MAGNIFIED

The visual stimuli that draw attention to women's bodies and create sexual tension around them are those that

- are flashy;
- are form-fitting;
- reveal a large area of skin (short clothing, plunging necklines);
- are impractical (shoes, hair length);
- are uncomfortable (shoes, underwire bras);

- involve a risk of overexposure (short, open-ended clothing like dresses and low-cut necklines);
- require lots of maintenance (hairstyle, makeup, and body-hair removal); and
- alter the body's true physiological appearance (bras, shoes, makeup, hair removal, plastic surgery, etc.).

But to be clear: I'm not arguing these practices should not exist, nor that women should not adopt them.

Nothing I have described above is inherently "bad." Wearing long hair, trading comfort for aesthetic appeal, applying makeup, exposing one's skin — none of these behaviours is wrong, superficial, or sexist by default. They are all perfectly valid and rational choices. Fashion can be a form of expression and a symbol of belonging, a sign of rebellion and way to break with previous generations (e.g., teenagers whose style shocks their parents). They can also be the opposite: a manifestation of conformity, a way of showing that we follow society's codes and we aren't going to make waves. These practices can also be about seduction, which isn't necessarily a bad thing.

Given the sexist differences we have observed, we could argue women should simply opt out and put an end to the inequality. But doing so would overlook the fact that we could easily argue the opposite: men could very well start adhering to these fashions and customs, too. They could, after all, wear skirts and dresses, put on makeup, shave their legs, wear tight clothing, and dye their hair blond. Why not?

A FEW CLARIFICATIONS

There will always be men who wear clothing that defies the conventional trends. But these men are considered "effeminate" or "eccentric." The same goes for women who wear typically masculine clothing; we call them "butch" or "tomboys," or even say they have "let themselves go."

Some fashions allow cisgender men and women to play with styles that are not generally associated with their sex. But when this happens, people usually display enough of the characteristics associated with their own gender that we can easily tell the difference. To date, our culture has never accepted a truly lasting, non-gendered fashion.

Fashion and its codes are not inherently problematic. *What is problematic, what is sexist, is when they are drawn along gendered lines.* Women are conditioned to follow a pre-determined path within a patriarchal culture, where femininity is associated with sex, beauty, superficiality, and, in the face of any transgression, immorality, while men are required to conform to a different, though no less compelling, code.

The problem is that we separate the sexes, telling them they must present their bodies differently because we treat them differently. We refuse to grant them the same symbolic value, sexually and politically.

Finally, contrary to what we like to believe, gender-based fashion differences are not intended to accommodate the real anatomical differences that exist between the sexes. They are artificial markers, created to meet cultural expectations.

These fashion differences have numerous consequences for real bodies, which we end up mistaking for "innate" behaviours and attitudes. We end up associating clothing-related mannerisms with women: shoes can cause changes to our gait, skirts restrict our movements, we sit differently in pants and play with hair differently depending on its length. Our attire can have a positive or a negative impact on our general well-being. Fashion affects our behaviours in both large and small ways. These differences constitute what we have come to call "feminine" and "masculine."

FEMININITY: A GENTLE FORM OF OBJECTIFICATION

> Vain trifles as they seem, clothes have, they say, more important offices than to merely keep us warm. They change our view of the world and the world's view of us.
> — Virginia Woolf, *Orlando*

Objectification is the art of seeing or interacting with a woman in a manner that ignores her humanity. We erase her personality, desires, and free will in order to focus solely on her physical appearance. Her body becomes an object to act on, irrespective of her emotions, thoughts, fears, and desires.

In the grossest caricature of objectification, a woman is literally treated as an object of consumption. A woman-table. A woman-steak. A woman-beer.

We often cite objectification when examining advertisements intended to sell a product. But the phenomenon has a much wider reach. Objectification occurs in art, fiction (think of the countless movies where the woman exists to serve the fantasy of the male hero), and pornography (no example needed).

And objectification goes well beyond images and fiction. Simply introducing or interacting with a woman in such a way that ignores her own wishes is to objectify her. A woman who has been assaulted or sexually harassed has been objectified. The offender is wholly unconcerned with the victim's emotions, which allows him to treat her as a tool he can use as he wishes, without consideration of or respect for her humanity.

Desiring someone does not equal reducing that person to a thing. The difference between the two lies in understanding that the object of our desire might not desire us in return. That person might not necessarily want what we want, and we cannot ignore this fact. When we take these circumstances into account, we act respectfully toward the person we desire.

Objectification is a way of submitting a woman to a man's desires and completely disregarding what she wants for herself. It is acting as though the only thing she could desire is to fulfill a man's needs.

Every object requires a subject. This acting subject — the man — is the only one with real importance. He is considered a human being, with goals, wishes, and desires.

Style is the primary vector of objectification when it comes to gender division. It is what puts women's bodies on display — so that we come to see their image as what defines them — and brushes men's bodies aside. Men are defined by their personality, words, and actions, not by their appearance. This results in an imbalance of power that benefits men.

Women's fashion systematically places them in the role of object. A woman is fundamentally decorative. Her purpose, her raison d'être, is to attract attention by magnifying her body — deforming it, colouring it, moulding it, concealing it, and exposing it.

Men's fashion is much more pragmatic. Instead of attracting attention to the body, it neutralizes it.

Our society believes that men are too respectable to have their bodies put on display, though it has no problem demanding that women turn on the fireworks in order to entertain and excite.

As a vector of objectification, fashion greatly impacts the way men perceive women — and how women perceive themselves. And by influencing how we use our bodies, fashion also has an impact on our sex drive.

Women's fashion constantly exposes heterosexual men to visual stimuli that draw their gaze to the female body. The stimuli men put forward, on the other hand, don't give women much to work with.

A woman must make a conscious effort to sexualize a man, since doing so runs counter to the prevailing culture. Our society does not predispose women to look at men sexually. Yet men don't even have to lift a finger: in our culture, the female body is already eroticized. Men's libido is constantly primped, pampered, and massaged.

Predictably, the consequences of this double standard are at odds with each other: men's sex drives are continuously stimulated, while women's are grossly ignored.

Indeed, the mass objectification of women is so powerful that instead of checking out men, women's attention is often directed at other women.

I was a teenager when I first realized this. I was riding the bus to school, watching the other girls get on, and noticed that I was more interested in them than the boys. It was the same thing every time I walked into a room: I would always check out the women instead of the men. When I became aware of it, I started scrutinizing what everybody else was looking at. Unsurprisingly, men looked women over — some carefully, unreservedly, and without shame, as if trying to publicly demonstrate their virility. But I also noticed that, like men and like me, women checked out other women. Women especially notice other women. In other words, men look at women and women look at women. Everyone, it seems, has their eyes trained on women.

We expect men to enjoy and be excited by a woman's appearance, and we expect women to see themselves through the lens of other women. After all, don't women look each other over as a way to compare?

The cliché would argue they're in competition with each other, and there's certainly merit to this. As women grow up in a world obsessed with their appearance, they need to see how they measure up, to know where they rank in men's eyes. The answer has a direct impact on the type of attention they will — or will not — receive.

But this "competition" isn't the only reason women observe each other. Simply put, women's fashion is more interesting than men's fashion. It is more visually stimulating, no matter who is looking. Moreover, women — like men — unconsciously internalize the notion that women are objects to size up, admire, or disparage (even when the gaze is directed at them).

Straight men develop a libido that corresponds with the mass objectification of women. They desire women, and they feed this desire by staring at them — a practice that is encouraged by female fashion. The circle is complete.

But straight women are out of step in terms of their sexual orientation. Since men's bodies are presented as uninteresting and thus ignored, women are more apt to be visually drawn to other women, even though they ultimately want to sleep with men. This is how women become autophiles, or sexually attracted to themselves.

Heterosexual women construct their sexual identity in contrast to what our culture sexualizes (women's bodies), and many end up being aroused by their own image or by projecting themselves onto other women. It is their own body that excites them, and above all, the sight of their body or that of another woman (in porn, for instance) desired by a man.

"Men look at women, and women watch themselves being looked at. This determines not only most relations between men and women, but also the relation of women to themselves," John Berger argued in the 1970s.[5]

Dubbed the "male gaze" by film critic Laura Mulvey,[6] the dominant masculine view of women colours all our perceptions, both on-screen and in real life, and has deep repercussions on female sexuality.

Women see men's desire as a detour, a type of psychological splicing used to compensate for the fact that they receive almost no sexual stimuli from men.

Women become aroused when men desire them. This narcissism may also provide a counterbalance for the fact that having access to a man's body (considered nonsexual by default) is not enough.

Let's take a classic scenario: a man and a woman want to have sex. They are attracted to one another, but the man is already more aroused because he has been receiving visual stimulation for hours. They find a room where they kiss and touch one another with their clothes still on, until it becomes too much and they start to undress. As the woman's shirt hits the ground, the man sees her bra — hiding her breasts but calling attention to her chest. Tension fans his desire; there is one final step before he can behold her naked. The mystery remains. But when the man takes off his shirt, the woman hardly skips a beat: she has seen male torsos in contexts as nonsexual as the pool or the beach, or even walking down the street in summer. But once her bra is unfastened, the man will have access to a part of her body that is reserved for intimacy.

When a woman removes her shirt, the eroticism it generates is not equal to the eroticism generated when a man removes his. To rise to her partner's level of excitement and compensate for her lack thereof, the woman must find a supplement of sexual tension; she must search her partner's eyes for the desire that seeing her breasts has provoked.

I use the breasts as an example here, but the same goes for the entire female body, which is culturally over-eroticized.

The woman's autophilia is dependent on the desire the man feels for her. This contrasts with her partner's desire, which functions autonomously the moment he has access to her body.

The result of this objectification is that women are just as, if not more, aroused by the female body than by the male body — even if straight women have little interest in sex with other women. This probably explains why women tend to be more "bi-curious" than men. Straight women watch lesbian porn and are more comfortable with inviting a partner of the same sex into a threesome. One study even reported that 82 percent of women react to sexual stimuli from both sexes.[7]

Practically every media outlet that mentions this oft-cited study interprets it as a sign of women's bisexuality. Incidentally, the study's lead researcher, Dr. Gerulf Rieger, has a similar interpretation. Rieger concluded that most women are either lesbian or bisexual, "even when they identified as heterosexual."[8] I feel this interpretation goes too far. The fact that our body reacts to stimuli does not mean we are necessarily attracted to the source (otherwise this would also mean that women are zoophiles, since studies have shown women become sexually aroused at the sight of other animals mating). Rieger's conclusion doesn't take into account the fact that women live in a society where the female body embodies sex — for both genders.

Still, it's interesting to consider that myriad sources of stimuli are able to arouse women. When I spoke with Meredith Chivers — one of the study's researchers and a woman whose work I greatly esteem (I met Chivers as part of my work on *Sexplora*) — she confirmed that women's response to stimuli does not mean they are bisexual. She pointed out that the discrepancy between stimuli that aroused participants based on their sexual orientation only pertained to straight women, not gay men. If we believe women respond with arousal to other women's bodies because the feminine form is highly sexualized in our culture, why wouldn't homosexual men respond similarly?

Consider the following:

- Gay men react to the male body
- Lesbians react to the female body
- Straight men react to the female body
- Straight women react to both male and female bodies

Why does the sexual orientation of straight women seem more malleable than that of other groups? Why are gay men indifferent to sexualized representations of the female body? My hypothesis is that the homosexual sex drive — for men or women — develops on the fringes of the dominant sexual culture, and this is obviously not the case for heterosexual women. A gay man doesn't respond to women's bodies, even if the equation "woman = sex" shapes our customs, since he actively rejects this idea by virtue of his sexual orientation. But heterosexual women do not reject the dominant sexual model. They adhere to it psychologically, because they have a social role to play in it. The result is that the "man = sex" equation operates on them, as per their sexual orientation, but the "woman = sex" equation also operates on them, as per the propaganda that encourages them to take part in the dominant sexual model.

There is one final negative consequence of gendered fashion that can be particularly damaging: women's ongoing efforts to care for their body and face distance them from their true appearance. High heels add height, belts flatter the figure, makeup camouflages blotchy skin, straighteners tame unruly hair, bras make breasts appear fuller and larger. It all widens the gap between a woman's self-image and what she really looks like. Even though on some level she is aware of the reality, it can be difficult not to believe that other women come closer to the sublime image they project.

A woman *knows* that she doesn't get up in the morning wearing the face she presents to the world. And this truth may cause her to feel like a fraud. For men, it is a non-issue: their private and public appearance does not vary greatly. With men, what you see is what you get.

Women may come to fear having men they have seduced see them as they are naturally. After sleeping together for the first time, a woman might feel anxious about the following morning, when her partner will see her unvarnished image. Will he still find her sexy? This additional pressure that is thrust onto women can affect their relationship to sex and intimacy.

When we look closely at the sex drives of men and women, it is impossible to ignore how we grossly objectify women and place men's desire at the centre of the social world. From birth, gender division assigns women a decorative role, which they must assume in order to stimulate men. And this expectation is a one-way street; no such demand is made of men.

We like to think that men are naturally driven to find women's bodies desirable. But if this is the case, why do women have to work so hard to please? Why should the "desirable" body type be so rare? And if, as we also believe, women's sexual appetite is not as instinctive as men's, wouldn't it make sense that men — like male peacocks displaying their colourful tail — should have to work harder to attract their attention?

In reality, men's libido is not so instinctive. On the contrary: it is thoroughly and continuously nurtured by our culture. The female sex drive, on the other hand, is neglected. It must be self-generated and self-perpetuating. Men, after all, are far too important to be sexualized for female desire.

5

The First Sex:
Teaching Women Not to Objectify Men

All animals are equal, but some
animals are more equal than others.
— George Orwell, *Animal Farm*

Sexual desire informs our choices and interests in unexpected ways. It is how we condition this desire — limiting or fuelling it according to a person's social identity — that influences social structure and keeps the patriarchal system alive.

Up to this point, we have examined the cumshot principle through the lens of femininity, or how women bear the responsibility for attracting and receiving men's desire. But women aren't passive targets, even though we perceive them as such. They feel desire, too. Yet, because our culture presents sex as a demeaning act, and because men mustn't be demeaned, we keep women's libidos in check so men aren't encumbered with requests for sex. We teach women that men are not there to elicit or satisfy desire. Rather, a man is someone to respect, someone to fall in love with.

As a result, to be attracted to a man, many women need to feel something that goes beyond the physical. These are the women who project themselves into a relationship from the moment they meet someone they like. They find it difficult to stick to carnal desire when taking a lover.

These women did not miss out on the sexual revolution; they are simply incapable of seeing their partners as anything but a person in their own right. And it would be hypocritical to claim this surprises us, given how we subjectify men.

What does it mean to subjectify someone? Subjectification is the opposite of objectification. It is another component of the cumshot principle, which presents sexual attraction as a unidirectional urge that originates with the man and is directed onto the woman. The man is the narrator and the subject of our sexual fantasies.

In our culture, men are systematically subjectified: they are both represented and recognized as complete beings.

Desiring someone who is subjectified means being attracted to their entire being: their personality, character, interests, talents, and dreams. And because this attraction goes beyond the physical, it is difficult to sexualize a subject — a man — without falling in love with him. Desire becomes all encompassing. And when that happens, it turns into something of a crush, or love, or at the very least, affection.

To avoid this "love risk," a woman seeking sexual satisfaction might sleep with men she is attracted to physically but not emotionally. Doing so could, however, stand in the way of sexual desire since she has been conditioned to value the man as a whole. If everything about a man save his physical appearance turns a woman off, she will likely have a hard time getting wet.

On the flip side, most men will have no problem getting an erection if a woman excites them, but doesn't really interest them as a person. After all, they have been trained to separate a woman's personality from her appearance.

Our patriarchal system does not tolerate women who treat men so cavalierly. Men must not be seen as sex objects: their integrity must be respected and they must be listened to. Placing too much value on their appearance jeopardizes their power in society.

We don't want to sexualize men's bodies in public spaces, since this might lead to an equal balance of power between genders.

Exposing women's bodies on billboards, in pop culture, and on the street would not be inherently sexist if society did not encourage sex segregation. Yet tradition dictates we expose women's bodies and conceal men's bodies without intending to create sexual tension by doing so — and *that's* truly sexist.

"To live in a culture in which women are routinely naked where men aren't is to learn inequality in little

"BUT WHAT ABOUT MEN?"

When we talk about how women's bodies are objectified in public spaces, someone invariably points out
that men are treated similarly, notably in underwear advertisements. This is, of course, true — but we cannot
compare the instrumentalization of the genders, since
sexualized images of men appear within a larger context of male subjectification. Psychology researchers in
the United States and Belgium presented participants
of both genders with images of attractive people in
undergarments or bathing suits. They observed that
participants perceived only the women as objects, not
the men.[1] In other words, even in the few instances
where men are sexualized, they are still subjectified.

ways all day long," wrote Naomi Wolf in her 1990 best-
seller, *The Beauty Myth.*[2]

It is for this reason that fashion puts so little emphasis on men's bodies. We don't want women paying too
much attention to men; otherwise, men would have to
make sustained efforts to maintain and improve their
appearance. This would take time, energy, and money
— resources they would no longer devote to consolidat-
ing prestige and power. In public spaces, women should
not be encouraged to stare at sexy men, check out a
passing hunk, or ignore aging men with their sagging
bodies. They must instead be indulgent and look past
a man's physique to consider the set of criteria directly
linked to the place men hold in society.

We condition women to be attracted to

- a man's sense of humour and talents (they are expected to entertain);
- a man's material possessions (they must make more money);
- a man's intelligence (they produce knowledge);
- a man's professional success (they must hold greater prestige than their partner); and
- a man's power (they are supposed to run society).

Meanwhile, we fail to condition men to be attracted to these same qualities in women.

Sexual attraction directly impacts our ambitions and dreams. When we desire others, we are pushed to gain skills they consider important. So if men do not value women's power, money, or sense of humour, these qualities become largely irrelevant. Men, however, continue to cultivate these same qualities to attract women. The status quo is maintained.

Subjectifying men provides them with "sexual immunity." This immunity reinforces and secures both their power in society and their power during courtship rituals. We accord men the respect a person deserves, but we don't always do the same for women. Considered objects by default, women must work to extricate themselves from mass objectification by painstakingly convincing men of their worth outside of sex.

We could rebel against the injustice of the woman-object/man-subject dynamic. We could declare that women should start "acting like men" — that women should objectify men — in order to reverse the trend. But it isn't that simple.

It isn't just that women are "too empathetic" to treat men as objects; the entire process is difficult to set in motion. Objectification is a mass movement propelled by culture. For centuries, men have enjoyed cultural artifacts, made by men, that depict women as objects. And our culture continues to be produced in large part today by men using their male gaze to instrumentalize women.

Men objectify women almost automatically, since the process is already at work around them. It's simply the norm. Both genders are conditioned to accept their roles: women as objects, men as subjects.

But when it is a question of objectifying each other, men and women are on unequal footing. A woman who wants to instrumentalize a man for sexual purposes has to make a conscious effort to oppose the prevailing culture. It's complicated, and it's a lot of work. Objectification is a collective process, not a dynamic operating between individuals.

While it is nearly impossible to have a woman shift her perception of a man from subject to object, the opposite is not true: men often find themselves treating women as whole people, though they may have started out as objects in their eyes.

Though men learn to dissociate a woman's body from her person, the process isn't always triggered when it comes to the women close to them. It may not be a knee-jerk reaction, but we tend to humanize people we regularly interact with, and come to value these individuals for all sorts of reasons unrelated to appearance.

Within the context of heterosexual courtship, the man sees the woman-subject as a companion: a wife, partner, girlfriend — or a woman who can fill these roles. If a man deems a woman "worthy," she earns the right to be considered a multi-dimensional human being; her words, desires, and preferences must be respected. This woman is what we'd call *girlfriend material.*

Indeed, many men categorize women into either *good* (the subjectified) or *slutty* (the objectified).

Women are classified depending on whether or not a man feels they deserve respect. The distinction is completely subjective — one man's good woman may well be another man's slut, and vice versa. A man may initially objectify a woman he finds sexy, only to begin subjectifying her (and expressing interest in all aspects of her person) once he starts falling for her. But, don't forget, the woman must first prove she is girlfriend material.

Let's explore how some men perceive women to be "just a piece of ass." The idea is absurd; women do not exist solely to offer men sex. They have temperaments, personalities, and interests, which are not necessarily aspects of themselves on "offer." Many men refuse to acknowledge these dimensions if they judge a woman unworthy. Yet this won't stop men from wanting access to the ass in question, since they are conditioned to view a woman's body as separate from her personality.

We'd like to believe we've long since outgrown this line of thinking, but we haven't. In an American study that explored the sexual behaviours of college students, young men admitted that if the girl they liked had sex with them too quickly — on the first or second date — they were less likely to consider her girlfriend material.[3] This rationale goes back to the purity imperative: if a woman does not prove her purity by abstaining from sex, she risks losing the man, along with the prospect of building a relationship together. By agreeing to sex, she becomes less appealing. Sex has sullied her and reduced her to just a receptacle for cum.

CAN WOMEN OBJECTIFY MEN?

When Canadian Prime Minister Justin Trudeau was elected in 2015, he made headlines around the world, many of which highlighted his sex appeal.

"Is Justin Trudeau the sexiest politician in the world?" wrote British publication *The Mirror*. The Philippines' *Daily Inquirer* described the prime minister as the "sexiest leader in the free world." American website Jezebel declared him "non-controversially fuckable."

Many people were outraged in the wake of such reports, denouncing the lusty comments women were splashing across social media as "objectifying" Canada's prime minister.

Was Justin Trudeau treated as a sex object?

I said it before and I'll say it again: finding someone sexy is not the same thing as objectifying them.

Sexually objectifying someone means seeing them as a one-dimensional being whose main purpose is to submit to sex. It means believing the individual in question has no personal goals other than to arouse sexual desire in us. And it involves denying the object of our fantasy exists the moment he or she disappears from our lust-filled vision.

Finding someone sexy means attributing a sexual charm to them while recognizing they are a complex individual with a will of their own. And desiring someone has no bearing on how this person should act toward us. When a person finds another person attractive it should not be demeaning — their desire should not humiliate the other's, undermine their credibility, diminish their importance, or pressure them into exposing their body or allowing themselves to be used.

Women's salacious comments about Trudeau can certainly be considered vulgar or inappropriate. It is safe to bet, however, that most do not fit into a context of objectification and have not damaged the prime minister's credibility or importance.

Might Trudeau have read these comments and felt objectified? Possibly.

This is where we must make a distinction between objectification on an individual versus a collective level.

Determining whether someone is objectified on an individual level is an exercise in subjectivity. We cannot do the labelling, cannot say, "You are being objectified." No one can judge another's objectification, since by definition the term involves an individual perception.

One might argue that strippers are objectified because they expose their bodies to stimulate arousal in exchange for money. But if a woman makes a conscious and informed choice and feels comfortable and respected in her line of work, she is not objectified: she is exercising free will. Saying otherwise risks dictating how she should feel and behave, using our own values as a benchmark. It disregards her emotions and subjective experience. In other words, this logic is just another form of objectification.

We cannot arrive at any sort of conclusion by evaluating an interaction from afar. While this doesn't mean objectification is not taking place, we must also take into account how the person receiving the request for sex perceives the situation. We can only analyze a culture of objectification from afar when the dynamic becomes systemic — hence my emphasis on the term *mass objectification*.

When women talk about their attraction to Justin Trudeau, their comments don't bear the same weight as a man who whistles at a woman in the street. Tradition would argue that what happened to the Canadian prime minister is unusual, while what happens to the woman in the street is to be expected.

Objectification requires a dynamic of domination. In our culture, it is men who dominate women. So even if a particular woman can sexually instrumentalize a man she dominates (e.g., a rich woman who buys sexual favours from a poor man forced to prostitute himself, who feels he has been used or disrespected), on a societal level it is still men who culturally instrumentalize women. Male desire governs a woman's experience in all sorts of ways and in all types of spheres, from fashion choices to rape culture.

Yes, a man can feel objectified by a woman. But no, as a gender, men are not collectively objectified. Women are.

PORN DOES NOT OBJECTIFY MEN

Some sexologists or porn experts contend that pornography objectifies men just as much as it does women. Most of the time, they argue, the camera focuses only on a man's penis while the rest of his body is kept off-screen, similar to how women's bodies are fragmented in advertising. True, men are not as seen and heard in pornography as women are. But how men are presented is actually a very effective manner of subjectification: it isn't the actors being subjectified, it's the men watching the screen. Producers keep the camera trained on the actresses for the pleasure of their male audience. These are the spectators that matter — porn fuels men's sexual orientation (presumably straight), the fetishization of the female body, and men's ability to mentally project themselves into a scene. We want the male viewer to feel as if the anonymous penis on-screen were his own. He is offered a story of which he is the hero. In short, he becomes the subject.

Expressions of desire can be enjoyable to hear when the attention is wanted. The problem, however, is that we can't always predict whether or not our advances will be well received. So, to avoid objectifying our partner, we need to give them the opportunity to express their feelings of mutual desire, aversion, or indifference.

The idea is not to create a world in which no one can express desire: a woman can passionately want to be wanted passionately.

Feeling someone's eyes on our body can be exhilarating, even when the attraction is not mutual. Feeling desired is an aphrodisiac. For some women, it represents power or a form of gratification, and some use it for material gain (through sex work or by dating a man who can support them) or to boost their self-esteem. There are men who envy this sexual power. They argue that it counterbalances all the other privileges men benefit from. "Women can't complain about being underpaid or underrepresented in Parliament because they have something we don't: sex appeal!" This is clearly untrue and manipulative. Nonetheless, there are women who use men's desire to their advantage.

We can concede the injustice; men do not have access to this power.

Forbidding women to view the male body as an instrument of pleasure not only limits their sex drive, but also penalizes men, who are denied the heady pleasure of being desired by strangers who simply find them sexy.

Similarly, sex segregation denies men the pleasures of dressing up, admiring themselves in the mirror, and feeling eyes glued to their bodies. When men are confined to the role of hunter, they lose out on the joy of giving themselves up to the pursuit, of being dominated by a sexual partner who "knows what she wants." They are denied the pleasures of autophilia.

GROOMING TEENAGERS

We have seen how the objectification of women parallels the subjectification of men, and how patriarchal societies maintain these mechanisms. I would be remiss if I didn't mention another cog in the wheel, one we almost never bring up: the way we groom young girls who develop an attraction to boys once puberty hits.

In early adolescence, girls naturally begin to sexualize boys. Yet society actively encourages them to censure their attraction by mocking their behaviour.

Adults deliberately humiliate teen girls who are too "boy crazy." When I was younger, I remember the adults around me sighing with exasperation as I drooled over videos of the Backstreet Boys dripping with rain, shirts unbuttoned.... "The Backstreet Boys are all gay," one of them said to me at some point, clearly hoping to discourage my infatuation with these heartthrobs.

Generation after generation, some things never change. One Direction, Justin Bieber, Elvis Presley, NSYNC: girls go wild, and adults roll their eyes.

More than just ridiculing this behaviour, adults and media outlets continue to disparage young men who break into the pop scene using their sex appeal. The furious anti-Bieber movement of the early 2010s was completely irrational. Why did adults so aggressively despise a musical talent that was not in any way aimed at them? Why was there so much contempt for the young singer? Were adults really so proud that their musical tastes differ from those of a fourteen-year-old girl?

The teen girl craze for boy band members is the closest we come to objectifying men. These boys are fodder for fantasy — they are meant to excite in the same way that women in porn feed boys' sexual urges. But while the latter seems normal, we are appalled when girls lust after the former. It proves a threat to the established order: teenage girls are meant to be desired, not feel desire themselves.

The situation is all the more disturbing given that girls develop a sex drive at an age when society expects them to accept their role of object. After all, patriarchy needs women to learn how to prioritize men's sexual urges while they are still young, malleable girls.

Instead of exhibiting their feverish desire for the members of One Direction, girls are forced to keep their sexuality in check to maintain the fantasy of transgression, to focus on developing a beauty ritual that stimulates men's libido without expecting anything in return.

We ridicule cultural products that specifically target teenage girls' sex drives, and we humiliate these girls in an attempt to stifle their popstar crushes. We shame them until they fall in line.

Teens have active sex drives, and the entertainment industry knows it: they make a fortune marketing boy bands and other male stars to teenage girls. But the rest of society considers it preposterous that these girls should be crazed with desire. How immature can we be?

These practices remain an effective way to keep the cumshot principle alive and well.

6

The Holy Grail:
Heterosexual Sex and Psychological Treats

> My body is very attracted to your body,
> but when you speak my brain gets angry.
> — *The Mindy Project*

Birth control was democratized during the sexual revolution of the 1960s and 1970s. The widespread popularity of the pill and the condom made it possible to have "traditional" penis-in-vagina sex with a much lower risk of getting pregnant. As a result, sex became an activity with fewer repercussions, opening up a range of possibilities.

It was also during the sexual revolution that the institution of marriage began to flounder. Up to that point, institutionalized monogamy had been the only acceptable option — men and women had to be married in order to have sex — and this model endured for centuries.

Sex, previously synonymous with "marital duty" and "baby-making," became recreational. Since the sexual revolution, we can now consider sex to be an end in itself, an act dissociated from a relationship, a family, and love.

Today, we can sleep with someone without envisioning a future together. No marriage, no kids. We don't have to be in love to have sex. And if we want, we can even have sex and never see the person again. The once-unthinkable possibility of recreational sex is now a well-entrenched trope in today's pop culture: *Sex and the City*. Girl power. Fuck buddies. Just "seeing" each other. Booty calls. Open relationships. One-night stands. Tinder.

Today, separating sex from feelings is not only possible, but also desirable. It's a sign of women's liberation: "If I can sleep with a man without getting attached, it means I'm strong. I'm in control of my future, of my body." Having sex with no strings attached is, for many women, proof of independence.

To be sure, the romantic relationship remains an ideal. Whether it involves marriage or not, society is still built on the institution of the couple.

Thus, we don't think of these two goals — having sex without getting involved and searching for love — as being at odds with one another.

In fact, we generally assume that one precedes the other. We see both one-night stands and romantic relationships as different life stages. Everyone is expected to experiment with multiple partners as we actively search for "the one," the perfect person with whom to build a relationship and start a family. And if we miscalculate, if we realize we've chosen the wrong partner, we break up and start sleeping with other people again while we continue the search for our soulmate.

At first glance, this value system seems liberating for everyone. It does not discriminate based on gender, and it lets us enjoy life in whatever manner we see fit. It is seemingly neutral.

Except that it isn't.

Our system isn't neutral because it hinges on a stark divide in how the two genders perceive their quest. Although we are told it is possible to have sex with no strings attached and to also have romantic relationships, we encourage women to look for love and men to look for sex.

The two genders are given distinct goals when it comes to sex. Women are tasked with building a relationship, while men's mission is to get as much sex as possible, ideally with as many partners as possible.

From childhood we are led down these gendered paths, and by adulthood society judges us based on our ability to perform the expected roles.

Men and women are sent off seeking entirely different Holy Grails.

Today, a woman is better off pursuing the Holy Grail of Love since this quest allows her to sidestep being wholly objectified. Women who want to stop being viewed as prey, as simple targets, or even as "sluts," or who aspire to be regarded with respect and affection, must be "good girls." Doing so increases their value, since they have stayed "pure" — in other words, legitimate. Society will still objectify them, but their lovers won't. The desire to escape objectification pushes women toward the Holy Grail of Love, which is a corollary to the cumshot principle.

How are men and women encouraged to carry out their respective quests? There are all sorts of subtle and roundabout strategies. The most effective way is to persuade everyone that the opposite sex is utterly consumed by his or her own mission.

We convince women that men are sex-obsessed, just as we convince men that women are only looking for a relationship and love. This doublespeak becomes a self-fulfilling prophecy.

Clearly the mechanics of these two quests are not taught in the classroom. The messages are reproduced indirectly, yet continuously, across cultural platforms.

Take the man who is afraid of commitment, a cliché so widespread it fails to offend anymore. This stereotype is rampant in narratives featuring male-female relationships. He's the man every respectable rom-com heroine will end up infatuated with. He's Barney in *How I Met Your Mother*, Harvey in *Suits*, Eric in *Life as We Know It*, Mr. Big in *Sex and the City*. He's Christian Grey. He's James Bond.

The stereotypical man whose past is strewn with conquests, who keeps cheating on his wife, who is a commitment-phobe (only up to the denouement, when love eventually triumphs), represents virility in its purest form. The man who resists commitment is the alpha male, the man women drool over.

The man who doesn't want us is the one we need.

This archetype reinforces the old adage that women love bad boys, along with its equally crude counterpart, "nice guys finish last."

So, who is this bad boy? He exudes self-confidence, even arrogance, and treats women like numbers or objects to be consumed. He is the macho guy who exhibits dangerous and self-destructive behaviour, and he needs a woman to save him from himself by mothering him.

The nice guy, on the other hand, is characterized by his respect for women. He is looking to commit and lead a stable life, which is why women tend to turn their noses up at him.

Put simply, bad boys want sex but no relationship while the nice guys want a relationship (and monogamy).

What is puzzling about the idea that women have a weakness for bad boys is that these men purportedly make women unhappy. They don't give women what they "truly want," namely a relationship.

Of course, this hackneyed theory is not backed up with hard facts.

A 2003 study out of the United States aimed to test this "nice guy paradox." Forty-eight women between the ages of eighteen and twenty-three were asked to choose a partner for a fictitious woman from among men with three different profiles.[1] The first was the typical "nice guy": sensitive, attentive, kind. The second was a "real man": macho, insensitive, and self-centred. The third fell somewhere in the middle. In the second part of the study, another group of 194 women had to choose a man for themselves from among the same profiles. This time the women were given photographs of male faces, so they could take physical appearance into account when making their choice.

In both cases, most participants opted for the nice guy, with the neutral profile the runner-up. The bad boy was consistently the lowest ranked. Moreover, it turned out the women didn't think the nice guy seemed less exciting, funny, or sociable than the others.

Interestingly, participants' priorities changed depending on whether they were looking for a serious relationship or a more casual fling. In the first case, kindness was a priority. In the second, they didn't choose bad boys, but rather men who were more physically attractive, regardless of their personality.

We undoubtedly misattribute why we believe women love bad boys (and their behaviour). Just like men, women are attracted to beauty, and it is quite possible that good-looking men are the ones who tend to act like bad boys. In other words, a man with lots of sex appeal will often be taken for a bad boy: his popularity affords him the pick of the litter, which may predispose him to adopt associated behaviours (e.g., displaying unfailing confidence or not wanting to commit to a stable relationship). Put simply, it is not the "bad" variable which counts, but attractiveness (possibly correlated with the "bad").

The study reported that some participants did choose the "bad-boy" profile independent of the man's physical appearance, but these participants were in the minority.

Other studies have also explored the bad-boy stereotype. One demonstrated that women value altruism in men. Another found that when asked to choose the qualities they prefer, most women selected men who were sensitive and easygoing; very few picked men who were aggressive or hard to please.[2]

The cliché that women prefer difficult men who often treat them poorly does not hold much water, but is not completely false, either. Some women really do prefer this type of man. On several occasions I have interviewed women who openly admit to being attracted to bad boys. In my experience, these women often contrast the figure of bad boy to that of the "wimp." By this, they are really talking about a man who lacks personality. American researchers Geoffrey Urbaniak and Peter Kilmann agree; they conclude the expression "too nice" can be a polite euphemism for "boring."

Other women I have talked to admitted they like the challenge of a man who pushes them away and is stoic when it comes to love.

These are predictable reactions when we consider how the bad boy is presented in pop culture: he is the most desired, and therefore the most desirable. But the reactions are likely related to this female search for the Holy Grail. Women are socialized from an early age to believe finding a partner should be their primary life goal, and if the quest proves too easy it will bring an abrupt halt to an endeavour meant to occupy them for some time. The game ends too quickly. For many women, the intoxicating prospect of having the object of their desire fall at their feet and declare his undying love is a moment to be savoured, along with the fear that the jig could be up at any moment. If a man gets on his knees on the first date, he snuffs out the flame and derails the quest that motivated his conquest. It is the modern, feminized version of medieval courtship:

during the pursuit, the woman's desire should intensify little by little yet always remain partly unsatisfied.

Although some women claim to prefer bad boys, there's a much better explanation of the pervasive idea that "all women love a bad boy": Many men complain about their sexual and romantic failures, chalking it up to being "too nice." They feel that bad boys steal the show. Whether out of reflex or empathy, we often throw out a friendly, "It's because you're too nice!" Yet when a woman laments her lack of success with men, she is fed exactly the opposite: "It's because men find you intimidating!" The paradox is that women face rejection because they are too forceful, and men face rejection because they are not forceful enough. We use our difficulty conforming to gender stereotypes to justify our sexual misfortunes, which elicits the sexual dogma of dominant man/submissive woman.

Since men are indoctrinated to believe they should use trickery or elaborate strategies to entice women into their bed, they come to see sex as the ultimate life challenge.

Society promotes the notion that women get easily attached and want to shackle men with the old ball and chain. Men are led to believe that all women want babies, and that they are merely an accessory to this end (provided they have sufficient financial resources to support a family). And beware of marriage — the trap that affords women a right to alimony and/or child support in case of divorce! Charming, right?

For the men who subscribe to this narrative, the challenge isn't finding a partner — it's spreading a woman's legs without falling into the trap of love and relationships.

But for women, the trap is sex. We bombard them with cautionary tales of men who will do anything to get them in bed, who only want to use them, get them drunk, lie to them, and screw them before throwing them in a taxi at the end of the night. Charming, right?

I am aware that this is wildly stereotypical, but the dynamic of man-looking-for-sex and woman-looking-for-love colours our relationships. Obviously, women who go to great lengths to secure a man and sex-maniac men who essentially use women's bodies as sex toys for their own gratification are not representative of the population. But when we perpetuate the notion in popular culture — and come across one or two real-life examples — it is enough to generate mutual mistrust.

At times, all this may even push us to embrace these gendered clichés. When we assume accessing sex will be difficult, we become more avid hunters. Likewise, when we believe the man we are dating won't want to commit, a relationship becomes all the more important.

All of this takes us back to the essence of desire: feeling as if something is missing. To experience desire, we need to perceive a lack of something that will not be easy to secure. If a woman feels as though she can snap her fingers and make a man sexually available, her desire dissipates. Similarly, when a man takes it for granted that the girl he is seeing wants a relationship, he will be in less of a hurry to start one.

In both situations, the gendered Holy Grails inform our desire for sex or for love. These quests exert a force that both attracts and repels.

We cannot forget the arbitrary nature of this dynamic: these quests have only recently been split down gendered lines. Prior to the sexual revolution, sex and relationships went hand in hand.

BIOLOGICAL CLOCKS AND FEARING THE END OF THE WORLD

The biological clock metaphor is another effective way of impressing upon women the importance of the romantic relationship.

Women are told that their bodies are a time bomb, that their fertility decreases every year, while a man's fertility is unaffected by time. I described in Chapter 2 how we dramatize women's reproductive potential but ignore men's.

While this fear is grounded in reality (women cannot reproduce after menopause), the myth of the biological clock is painted in its most esoteric aspects as a primal urge, the body demanding a child and pushing women to desperately want to procreate. (I recently read an article about a woman who complained of menstrual cramps to her doctor, who responded by saying that her body was telling her it wanted a child.)

The narrative of the body demanding a child, combined with the threat of declining fertility, did not appear until women began flooding the workforce, explains American journalist and academic Moira Weigel in an essay published by the *Guardian*.[3]

The expression "biological clock" was coined in 1978 in a *Washington Post* article entitled "The Clock Is Ticking for the Career Woman." It has since been used countless times to caution women who put career ahead of family.

The image is a perfect — and gendered — call to order: "Ladies, never forget you have been put on this earth to marry and produce babies! You may well have a career and use contraception, but your true vocation is to conceive children."

It also, among other things, propagates the idea that reproduction is a woman's responsibility. We scare women by telling them to hurry up and find a man so they can make babies, or risk growing old and bitter, lonely, and unhappy. As if men don't need to find a partner if they want to have kids. As if they are indifferent to the idea of a family, and it is in their best interests to wait to start one. We also seem to think that even at a mature age they will always be able to find younger women to reproduce with (though the notion that older men all have access to a pool of young, single women is mathematically absurd).

Society insists that women are the ones who want children. There is a type of collective pressure to this end, and we expect women to subsequently pressure men on an individual level. Women therefore end up having to beg for commitment and children. In this way, we thrust family responsibility onto women, making it possible to demand sacrifices we would not expect from men.

And when we take the myth of the biological clock and tack on the popular belief that women are "natural multi-taskers," we prime them with the perfect ideological cocktail before placing the burdensome institution of family on their shoulders.

In fact, we expect women to come home after a day's work and begin another unpaid job — cleaning, cooking, and caring for the children. Since the woman wanted the family, she should be responsible for the upkeep it requires. And if a woman chooses to have a career in addition to being a mother, she shouldn't complain about being tired. Shouldn't ask her boss for special treatment. Shouldn't expect her partner to do an equal share at home. She asked for this life, after all!

Prioritizing family over career is a choice we only expect women to make.

Even the way we organize parental leave is suggestive. Parental leave plans assume women will spend most of the time home with the children, and that their partners will continue to work outside the home. In Quebec, where the plan is often touted as a model, 70 percent of men do not take advantage of the leave benefits.[4] This figure also matches the disproportionate share of household chores and childcare that women in Quebec often take on.

"You wanted kids, so take care of them."

These observations reflect another sacrifice only demanded of women: coddling their spouse and not receiving equal support in return. This is what we call *emotional labour.*

Coined in 1983 by sociologist Arlie Hochschild, the expression initially referred to work related to certain job sectors — mostly the service industry — where employees are expected to be cheerful, tolerant, warm, and deferential in order to provide an emotionally fulfilling experience. Think of bartenders and nurses: we expect them to express (or fake) certain emotions as part of their job.

But emotional labour exists in the private sphere, too. Take women who fake orgasms: we regard the act as terribly dishonest, yet many women feign climaxing to keep their partner emotionally satisfied, so that his enjoyment isn't tainted by the shame of not being able to satisfy *them*. Of course, men can fake an orgasm for the same reason. But women and men do such at disproportionate rates. According to a 2010 study from the United States, 28 percent of men and 67 percent of women have reported faking an orgasm during sex with penetration.[5] And while women cite wanting to boost a partner's self-esteem as the leading reason, men cite wanting to end a prolonged sexual encounter.

Faking an orgasm is just one of the many examples of the emotional labour carried out by women, who are seen as naturally more empathetic and affectionate than men. Women like to take care of their spouses, we tell ourselves. Men, on the other hand, provide resources, not comfort.

We also believe men don't have to make as much effort to convince their partners to stay in the relationship. Since men always have one foot out the door, women must bend over backward to keep them around. But women stay put, even when they aren't treated as well as they treat their spouse. Simply honouring them with a commitment should be enough to keep them invested in the relationship.

The myth of the biological clock induces women to accept these unfair situations. It also quells our collective fear of dying out, since people do worry that if women stop wanting children, we risk not being able to replace ourselves.

This same apprehension fuels homophobia and heteronormative discourse.[6] Some people believe that homosexuality represents a threat to humanity, since it poses a hurdle to populating the planet.

Many people who fear a population decline support a neoconservative chauvinistic agenda that suggests a declining birth rate will give competing nations the upper hand in terms of economics and military. We must make babies for the nation — to keep the economy on its feet! Yet we don't so much mean babies as we do little workers/consumers/soldiers.

This type of patriotic discourse is nothing new to me, but until recently I was under the impression that these people didn't broadcast their beliefs. That is, until I received this email, following a TV appearance, from someone who proposed I take a new direction as part of my work on sexuality:

> Beyond the quest for pleasure — a catchy, sexy topic to be sure — from the point of view of a white Francophone Quebecer, it's alarming how our culture will collapse from a failure to reproduce if we don't make drastic changes. French researchers have determined that the population replacement rate is an average of 2.4 children per woman.
>
> According to my research, we're at around 2.1 children in Quebec, including blacks,

Asians, Latinos, etc. Don't get me wrong, I have nothing against other cultures and races. But …

Just think, it took over four hundred years for white Francophone Quebecers to get out from under English rule and take charge of their lives. And if we don't do anything, we'll be wiped out of North America in just a few generations since other ethnicities naturally reproduce more quickly.

It's a shame.

I know this isn't your specialty, but once you make a name and reputation for yourself in the media, maybe you could address topics that are essential to our survival? […]

You see what I mean?

This fear, so openly expressed in the email, is very real. And women carry the burden of it. The image of the ticking biological clock and our fear of the end of humanity are ideologies working in tandem, conditioning women to see the couple as the locus of self-realization.

It is the couple, and not sex, that must remain women's Holy Grail, and as a result, their relationship to sex outside of this institution differs from men's.

PSYCHOLOGICAL TREATS

The problem with the quest for the Holy Grail among heterosexuals is that, even when fully aware of how absurd and stereotypical these gendered missions are, it is difficult not to fall into them. Because of the psychological treats.

A *psychological treat* is any advantage someone might get out of a given situation by virtue of their gender.

The ramifications for men and women who have sex outside the structure of a relationship differ considerably, which is why it is important to examine the costs and benefits for each gender, along with their underlying reasons.

As I argued earlier when I used Samantha from *Sex and the City* as an example, the archetype of the woman who has sex with multiple partners without falling for them is presented as an anomaly — she is wholly unlike the men who display these same behaviours. Samantha is a sort of anti-heroine, one female audiences are not required to identify with.

American comedian Amy Schumer has a similar stand-up persona: a drunk and slutty perpetual teenage alter ego who likes to party and sleep around. Like many comedians, Schumer stays in character for interviews. She plays a sex maniac who flees adult relationships so well that audiences have come to believe it to be her real personality.

But in more serious, intimate interviews, Schumer categorically dissociates from her character who is not, as one might think, a caricature of her own self. No, it is actually her anti-self. Amy Schumer, explains Amy Schumer, is a serial monogamist who has only had a single one-night stand in her whole life.

Of course, Schumer can be whoever she wants to be. I am using her example to illustrate how women tend to stick to the device of the Holy Grail, even when their public persona offers a picture of a woman on the fringes of sexual stereotypes.

It is difficult for a straight woman to think she has "scored" when she sleeps with a stranger, since the prevailing culture tells us that when it comes to sex, it is the man who gets something out of it. It is the man who deserves a high-five. He is the one to congratulate, to celebrate, because he has accomplished his mission. Not the woman.

The sexual revolution has done nothing to change the fact that sex gives value to men and takes it away from women. Several studies have confirmed this double standard, one of which reported that the anticipation of social reprobation following liberal sexual behaviour discourages women from participating in it.[7]

Society places a higher value on women who have not had sex (and who are therefore "pure") in order to discourage this behaviour.

An episode from the cult series *Gilmore Girls* brilliantly illustrates my point.[8] In one scene, Paris tells her friend Rory that she has just lost her virginity. The two teens are model students, both top of their class, who dream of getting accepted to Harvard. Seeking to intellectualize her sexual experience, Paris wants to know Rory's thoughts. While the girls are talking, Rory's mother, Lorelai, walks into the house and overhears their conversation. Paris asks Rory if she has slept with her boyfriend, and when Rory answers she has not, Lorelai is visibly relieved. She makes her entrance, pretending to have just come home, and acts unusually affectionate toward Rory — she even offers to take her shopping the next day. Lorelai is thrilled. "I've got the good kid," she boasts once the girls are out of earshot.

And this is how you get girls to connect "absti-nence" with "merit." Even worse, in the same episode we learn Paris has not been accepted to Harvard. Shocked, she goes off the rails while giving a speech that was sup-posed to be about education. In front of a full house, she reasons that her failure is due to the fact that she lost her virginity: "I'm being punished," she says. When Rory at-tempts to lead her offstage, Paris retorts that Rory, the virgin, will probably end up at Harvard.

We later learn that Rory has not only been accept-ed to Harvard, but to other prestigious universities, too. Clearly her success has nothing to do with her virginity — but thousands of teenage girls watched as Rory the virgin was rewarded by her mother and by life, in con-trast to an unlikeable and hysterical Paris, who loses her virginity and bitterly regrets it. Paris deems herself a slut and worries her boyfriend Jamie will stop loving her. Rory reassures her as best she can. In the closing scene, Rory is staring at all of her acceptance letters when Lorelai references what Paris said earlier: "Apparently, you're the biggest virgin in the world."

Virginity. Parental pride. Shopping spree. Academic success.

Our culture does not send men these kinds of mes-sages. We don't think sex reduces a boy's personal value, or that chastity augments it. If a boy stays a virgin, his parents don't tell him they are proud and don't reward him. At the very worst, when teenage male characters have sex, they are portrayed as bad boys taking advan-tage of girls' naïveté — as if sex did not directly concern them and it only affected the girls.

This image of the sexual encounter is so entrenched in our minds that men actually gain more from sex than women — the issue of pleasure completely aside. Even if the experience is disappointing, the man gets his gratification, since having sex is not considered damaging to his gender; in fact, it's highly encouraged.

Sexually active men feel good about themselves. They are doing what is expected of them. By virtue of their maleness, they must obtain sex from females if they want to be considered real men. This confirmation of manhood is a strong enough incentive to seek out sex. Desire for self-actualization is a strong motivator — it is, in fact, at the very top of Maslow's hierarchy of needs — and sex allows men to fulfill this need.

Even if a man does not tell his friends about a sexual encounter, the psychological satisfaction of having "scored" and therefore doing what is expected of him is enough to make him feel good.

I deliberately use the term "score" in reference to a sexual encounter, because that is what we are talking about: a goal, a points system. The same is not true for women: for them, sex is a zero-sum game where men always win the hand. There are no points for women who have sex. No matter what, a woman only scores if she can get a man to commit to her. Because culture runs deep.

I often find myself attracted to men from a strictly sexual point of view, no feelings involved. Sleeping with these men has frequently left me dissatisfied without me being able to articulate why. I wasn't looking for a relationship, so why didn't having sex leave me as fulfilled as my partners clearly were?

I chose those men. I was attracted to them, I managed to seduce them, and I brought them home. In short, I was the hunter. But from the very first kiss, the first caress, the situation seemed to reverse. My conquests would systematically take the lead. They seemed more excited by the prospect of sex, hornier, more eager to get down to business. They always wanted to go further, sooner, faster.

These men had internalized the idea that it was up to them to steer the ship to the bedroom, and I had internalized the idea that a woman should be passive. The men were more proactive, impatient, and even more ardent in their desire.

Despite my initial enthusiasm, the ensuing dynamic brought me back to "my place": I settled into the role of a woman who wants to slow things down.

My eagerness to score completely dissipated, in spite of myself. It is impossible to score with someone who is convinced he is the one scoring — especially in a culture that affirms his role as scorer.

In the end, the men I had wooed stole my psychological treat and swallowed it whole.

The idea is not to boast of my irresistibility; these experiences have nothing to do with my sex appeal. What happened between me and my partners did not have to do with our respective libidos, either. It had everything to do with gendered sexual dynamics.

When a woman has her psychological treat taken away, it discourages her from seeking future sexual experiences with no strings attached. And that brings us back to the paradigm of the Holy Grail of Love: for a woman, just wanting and getting sex is not satisfying in itself. The experience is nothing like the man's, who is always able to enjoy his self-actualization-flavoured treat.

There are obviously a host of situations where this dynamic is less clear-cut. Heterosexual women *can* feel as if they are the ones doing the scoring, despite what culture dictates. But after having spoken to several women on the subject, I know I am far from alone in these experiences.

And the way our peers react when we tell them about our sexual exploits also influences the way we see sex outside of the couple.

Social approval is a powerful enough incentive to positively reinforce the self-esteem of those on the receiving end. However, this approval is generally reserved for men, not women.

A woman who recounts the night's adventures to her girlfriends runs the risk of having her friends listen, only to turn around and wonder what she hopes will come out of it. Does she think the guy will call her back? Will they go out again? What does he do for a living? Are they compatible? These girls will insinuate that having sex is not enough. To sustain their attention, things can't end there. They want a fairy tale, a budding love story, as they were taught should happen to a woman. They are not impressed by sex, which is the easy part.

So. Contrary to what we claim, adventures in bed do not hold the same value for both genders. We tend to overlook the fact that men are entitled to the psychological treat, but not women.

Sex is not all about wanting to orgasm (this can be achieved through masturbation). Men derive psychological and even social benefits from sex, and it is high time to admit that the idea of "no strings attached" distorts our understanding of gendered behaviour.

And even if we look at sex solely through the lens of orgasm, men once again have more to gain than women.

1

The Orgasm Gap:
Aim for the G Spot and Miss the Target

I demand that I climax.

— Nicki Minaj

It is a well-documented fact: men come more than women when they have sex. Men literally have more orgasms.

According to an extensive American survey published in 2009, 91 percent of men reached orgasm during their last sexual encounter, compared to 64 percent of women.[1] When it was a question of climaxing during a hookup, men reached orgasm 44 percent of the time, compared to 19 percent of the time for women. In the context of a relationship, men came 85 percent of the time and women, 68 percent.[2]

Other studies show similar statistics. While results vary depending on the circumstances targeted by the researchers, they all reveal a significant gap between men and women when it comes to achieving orgasm.

There are numerous reasons a person might not orgasm during sex — and a sexual interaction can still be enjoyable without one. Not everyone considers climaxing to be an end in and of itself. But, that said, how can we explain the perpetual gap between the sexes? And why is it that in most cases it's the woman who has to accept the non-advent of an orgasm?

I'd like to demonstrate how our reductive ideas of sex, and of what defines having sex, lead to an orgasmic disparity between genders.

First, a man's pleasure and a woman's pleasure are not prioritized in the same way. The male orgasm is primordial — it is a sign of a successful sexual interaction. The female orgasm, however, is considered uncertain, even optional.

We are generally not as concerned with a woman's pleasure, and even less so when it comes to casual sex. "Both men and women question women's (but not men's) entitlement to pleasure in hookups but believe strongly in women's (as well as men's) entitlement to pleasure in relationships," note American researchers Elizabeth Armstrong, Paula England, and Alison Fogarty as part of a study on young people's hookups, dating, and relationships.[3] According to this logic, there are "two kinds" of female sexual partners.

Statistics on oral sex also illustrate the extent to which heterosexual partners prioritize male pleasure. A study published in 2016 in the *Canadian Journal of Human Sexuality* claims that 63 percent of men reported having received fellatio the last time they had sex, compared to 44 percent of women receiving cunnilingus.[4]

One 2009 study confirmed that for a first sexual encounter with a new partner, 55 percent of men received oral sex compared to only 19 percent of women.[5] It's no surprise, therefore, that men climaxed more than women.

Today we can be glad that women are in control of their own bodies, that they can sleep with whomever they want, whenever they want. But society still places more value on male pleasure than female pleasure. This is a major obstacle to the supposed total liberation of women's sexuality, and a clear indication that men's interests continue to be placed ahead of women's.

Indeed, many men — and women, for that matter — consider a woman's orgasm nonessential. We have developed this view without knowing why or how. And in some cases we might even think that if a woman does not climax, it's because her body is defective.

For the first few years I was sexually active, I, too, believed the reason I couldn't orgasm during sex was because there was something wrong with my body. Until it dawned on me that I wasn't getting the right kind of stimulation. It took me years to realize that what I had been taught about sexuality was only part of the story — and some of the information wasn't even true.

Like everyone, I had come to believe that the ideal sexual encounter involved penetration, followed by an in-and-out movement inside the vagina until the man ejaculated. The female orgasm, produced by this act, was supposed to occur during penetration.

Yet penetration is not a surefire way to get a woman to orgasm. Such is the case for only 25 percent of women, according to Elisabeth Lloyd, who analyzed thirty-two studies carried out over the past decades.[6] Lloyd found that only a percentage of women can attain orgasm "fairly often" during penetration.

Yet the data is incomplete, since most of the studies on female orgasm overlook one essential variable: multiple stimulation. Lloyd writes, "We are confronted with the sizeable task of knowing what exactly is an 'orgasm during intercourse with penetration.' Does a woman who achieves orgasm by penetration combined with manual clitoral stimulation count as a woman who achieved 'orgasm during intercourse with penetration'?"

These studies do not address how many orgasms were associated with stimulation other than vaginal penetration. The truth is, if we really want to understand which sexual practices are the most enjoyable for women, more research needs to be done. Current studies date back to the 1960s, 1950s, and even the 1930s — from a time when notions of sex and its accompanying taboos were very different.

To illustrate my point, let me refer back to my own experience. My rate of orgasm during penetrative sex is quite high. However, I know that this number is not directly related to vaginal penetration since I make sure my vulva and clitoris are being stimulated through contact with a man's pubis. If I had been a participant in one of these studies, there is a good chance I would have been part of the 25 percent of women who can easily achieve orgasm through vaginal penetration.

Yet it isn't my vagina, per se, that leads me to orgasm.

"What works for me isn't so much the 'penis-in-the-vagina' as much as the 'pubis-against-the clitoris,'" I explained on one 2015 episode of *Sexplora*, which was later uploaded to YouTube.[7]

Once the video aired, male viewers appeared confused:

"It would be great if guys could shift their erogenous zone to the pubis," one wrote cautiously. (Another pointed out that such a thing already existed: "It's called a penis.") "Is she seriously telling us that she'd rather orgasm with a girl?! What's 'pubis against clitoris' supposed to mean?" wrote another.

Clearly the knowledge that my orgasms weren't caused by vaginal penetration but rather from rubbing my clitoris against a man's pubis had unsettled these men.

To go back to the data, let's assume the 25 percent figure pulled from Lloyd's meta-analysis refers to women who always achieve orgasm solely through vaginal penetration. The next question is: how many of these women can repeatedly achieve orgasm through clitoral stimulation? Ninety percent.[8]

Hang on a minute.

We all know the clitoris exists, yet it doesn't get nearly as much air time as the vagina in our conceptions of sex. Our culture turns its nose up at both the clitoris and the vulva, which is another extremely sensitive organ.

Over the past few decades there has been a strong push to divide women into either "vaginal" or "clitoral" camps. Interestingly enough, everywhere we look, in movies, romance novels, or porn, women seem to get pleasure from the in-and-out motion of penetration. In our representations of sex, all women appear "vaginal." It almost seems like a conspiracy.

Sex education classes consistently overlook the role of the clitoris and vulva. In a 2009 questionnaire about the vulva, French high-school students managed to draw a diagram of the female reproductive organs (uterus and Fallopian tubes) but were unable to draw a vulva.[9] In essence, many teenagers had a better understanding of a woman's internal parts than her visible ones. Moreover, one thirteen-year-old girl out of two did not know she had a clitoris and only 16 percent knew its function (pleasure), compared to 35 percent of fifteen-year-old girls.

When it comes to masturbation, many women who self-stimulate the vulva and clitoris without any penetration believe themselves to be abnormal — they think other women masturbate using penetration.[10] Yet this is the case for only 5 percent of women, according to a 2005 web study of 27,000 women conducted by Dr. Catherine Solano.[11] The 2000 edition of *The Hite Report* confirms these observations.

I also believed I was abnormal for a long time because I wasn't able to orgasm vaginally. For ages, I tried to teach myself how to climax through vaginal stimulation, based on the model of female pleasure omnipresent in our culture.

I wasn't crazy: the belief that women must derive pleasure through penetration is deeply entrenched in our psyches, and we have Freud to thank for it.

The father of psychoanalysis decreed that women should learn to climax through vaginal stimulation. In the early twentieth century, he stoked a rivalry between vaginal and clitoral pleasure still present in popular culture today. Freud argued that vaginal pleasure should be superior in adult women; he considered clitoral pleasure to be immature. A woman had to wean herself from clitoral pleasure in order to develop a healthy sexuality. He writes:

> We are entitled to keep to our view that in the phallic phase of girls the clitoris is the leading erotogenic zone. But it is not, of course, going to remain so. With the change to femininity the clitoris should wholly or in part hand over its sensitivity, and at the same time its importance, to the vagina. This would be one of the two tasks which a woman has to perform in the course of her development, whereas the more fortunate man has only to continue at the time of his sexual maturity the activity that he has previously carried out at the period of the early efflorescence of his sexuality.[12]

Freud clearly did not base his theory on any empirical data. He was just mansplaining.

But the damage was done; one study published in 2008 (not 1908!) used Freudian theory to establish a link between vaginal orgasm and better mental health in women.[13] The findings astonished other researchers studying female sexuality, who were unable to reproduce the results and establish the same correlation in their own work.

According to a 2016 American study published in the *Journal of Sexual Medicine*:

1. The reported source of orgasm [clitoral or vaginal] was unrelated to orgasm intensity, overall sex-life satisfaction, sexual distress, depression, or anxiety.
2. Women who reported primarily stimulating their clitoris to reach orgasm reported higher trait sexual drive and higher sexual arousal [...].[14]

It should also be noted that researchers are questioning the entire existence of a G spot and vaginal orgasm, along with language conceived in recent decades to talk about the female orgasm. "The key to female orgasm are the erectile organs. The vaginal orgasm, the G spot, the G spot amplification, clitoral bulbs, clitoris-urethra-distal vagina complex, internal clitoris, and female ejaculation are terms that have no scientific basis. Female sexual dysfunctions are popular because they are based on something that doesn't exist, i.e., the vaginal orgasm," write Italian sexologist Vincenzo Puppo and his daughter, biologist Giulia Puppo, in a scathing publication.[15]

We keep saying how complicated female sexuality is, but could it be that we're the ones making it complicated?

Montreal researcher Jim Pfaus, whom I had the chance to meet on several occasions, does not disagree with Vincenzo and Giulia Puppo. He also rejects the vaginal/ clitoral orgasm dichotomy and believes the female orgasm can have different sources and is related to each woman's lived experiences. He and colleagues at McGill and Concordia universities argue:

> [T]he subjective experience of [the female orgasm] is not necessarily the same for each woman, and can even be different each time a woman has one. Those differences span physiology and psychology. They depend on the unique distribution of sensory nerves around the posterior clitoral complex and cervix, the integrity of the nerves that transmit those sensations into the spinal cord and/or directly to brain, and, perhaps most importantly, a woman's relative experience with sensory stimulation of one, some, or all of those regions being associated with orgasm.[16]

Scientific communities have finally allowed that women shouldn't have to choose between their (immature) clitoris or their (mature) vagina, and that other erogenous zones can trigger orgasm. Yet our collective obsession with the G spot that emerged in the 1980s reflects how the pro-vagina bias remains alive and well.

Why are we always urging women to "find their G spot"? Men can derive rectal pleasure through stimulation of the prostate — and while we never talk about this possibility among straight men, people have been going on about the G spot for three decades. So why don't we encourage men to find their P spot?

The entire genital area can potentially lead to orgasm for both men and women, and we often experience pleasure from stimulating a combination of these parts. It can be difficult for a woman to pinpoint exactly where her orgasms are coming from, just as it can be for men if we ask for a similar amount of precision. No doubt they will say the penis — but what part? The base? The glans? The foreskin? The corpus cavernosum? We don't ask men to determine whether they are "glansial," "cavernosial," or "foreskinial" because our conception of sexuality has a deep respect for the penis in its entirety. We don't ask men to choose between the sources of pleasure on their penis.

People who claim that women derive pleasure first and foremost from the vagina are forgetting one disconcerting fact: the vagina is not a terribly sensitive organ. This doesn't mean that contact with certain internal body parts surrounding the vagina or the pressure felt by the introduction of a penis cannot produce pleasure. Nevertheless, the vaginal walls themselves are not designed for optimal sensations, since they have very few nerve endings.

So which female body parts contain the most nerve endings? The vulva and, especially, the clitoris.

Another fact rarely taken into account is that the vulva and penis both develop from the same tissue inside the womb. They are homologous organs, which means they have a common underlying anatomy. Both have a glans protected by a foreskin; the vaginal lips correspond to the scrotum, and the vestibular bulbs beneath the skin of the small lips are similar to the spongy tissue of the penis. So why do we maintain that the vagina is the female equivalent of the penis, when biology would indicate it is actually the vulva?

I am not trying to invalidate the fact that some women prefer their vagina to be the main source of orgasms. I love my own, I can assure you, and my goal is not to refute other women's sexual experiences.

I would, however, like to point out how problematic it is that pop culture continues to depict women deriving most of their pleasure from their vagina — that it is this part of their anatomy that defines their sexuality more than anything else.

I want to emphasize how holding the vagina in higher regard over the clitoris, as per Freud's model, continues to colour our notions of female sexuality, and wrongly so.

Philippe Brenot, a French author who writes a lot about sexuality, recently confided to me that he hates how so many therapists continue to draw on this outdated theory, "even though Freud himself would have a different view today."

If we want to combat the unjust orgasm gap that persists between men and women, we need to stop focusing on the vagina at the expense of the vulva.

We can't keep thinking the orgasm gap is here to stay, especially since it is largely a result of the way we fundamentally view having sex — i.e., through vaginal penetration.

Once again, I am not arguing that penetration should fall by the wayside, or that women don't or shouldn't enjoy it. I'm only saying we need to stop presenting it as standard practice and arguing penetration is the "normal" and "right" way to orgasm.

THE IMPORTANCE OF THE VULVA

When we talk about the critical role of the clitoris, for many people the takeaway is that it must be continuously stimulated in order to induce pleasure. Yet the organ's sensitivity may not always work in its favour; many women find direct and intensive stimulation generates sensations that are too strong to be arousing. It would be like focusing on stimulating just one part of the penis: the glans. Such a thing would be unimaginable! There is general consensus that the entire penis should be stimulated. Well, the same goes for the vulva. The clitoris — like the glans — is packed with nerve endings, but stimulating other parts of the organ can also bring a woman to orgasm.

Let's examine the reasons we continue to insist on sexual pleasure that passes through the vagina. Why on earth do we place such value on this part of the female anatomy, both in fantasy and in practice? Three elements explain the pro-vagina bias: a puritanical vision of sex education, ordinary sexism, and naive romanticism.

A PURITANICAL VISION OF SEX EDUCATION

Sex has been a taboo subject for centuries, but at some point we do need to educate the younger generation about the birds and the bees. It can be tempting to skim over the topic. Most of the time, adults and educators stick to explaining sex-related risks (STIs, unwanted pregnancies, etc.). In other words, we tend to focus on the strictly reproductive aspect of sexuality — the least compromising aspect.

Where do babies come from? That is the question.

Our instrumental view of sex prompts us to explain everything through the lens of procreation. And since female pleasure plays no role in reproduction, it often takes a back seat in the classroom. To make a baby, all you need is a penis that ejaculates into a vagina. That's all there is to it.

When sex is viewed through this lens, the clitoris is reduced to a useless little organ. If we learn to see sex as "the reproductive act," it becomes normal, even logical, to completely ignore the vulva.

Reducing sex to a purely reproductive dimension only reaffirms the most conservative and puritanical vision of what it can be.

But humans do not always want to reproduce, nor is it always in their best interest to reproduce when they have sex. In fact, most of the time they want to *avoid* getting pregnant when they make love.

"But that's nature for you — that's the whole point of sex." I get that a lot, to which I reply, "Life isn't just about nature." It's also about building connections.

In addition to its reproductive purpose, sex also serves to create social bonds. It brings people together; it is a social activity that helps forge alliances, which are critical to human survival.

Sex is often about achieving a goal completely unrelated to reproduction, such as boosting self-esteem, attracting a partner, establishing a relationship, defining or reaffirming a bond, getting a psychological treat, and so on.

This would partly explain the existence of homosexuality — and not just with humans. Homosexual relations abound in nature. Animals of the same sex can show signs of affection, woo each other, and help each other masturbate. These practices have been observed and documented in hundreds of species.

A 2015 study on homosexuality appeared to conclude it was an adaptive form of sexuality as it increased alliances and emotional ties between members of a group.[17] "Homoerotic behaviour appears to play a role in promoting social bonds," explains researcher Diana Fleischman.

Long considered sexual deviancy, pathology, and even an imitation of heterosexuality, it is only once we stop regarding homosexual behaviour through this absurd lens that we begin to fundamentally question the purely reproductive role of sex. And this is likely one of the reasons homosexuality scares heterosexuals: it holds the current puritanical discourse on sex up to its contradictions.

Even if we disregard Fleischman's theory on homosexuality, we cannot deny that a large number of heterosexuals look for and practise sexual behaviours that do not lead to reproduction. Oral sex, anal sex, masturbation…. These behaviours, which are also observed among animals, have long been considered deviant. (As an interesting aside, note that "nasal sex" has been observed among dolphins in the Amazon River; they penetrate each other's blowholes, the opening on their head that allows them to breathe.)

When we stop viewing sex as a solely reproductive act, it makes us responsible for our own fantasies. Because in a culture that views sex as taboo, it suits us to imagine ourselves victims of an uncontrollable hormonal force that drives us to want to stick penises into vaginas.

This reductive view is a sort of compromise we make so that we can indulge in sex and still regard it as shameful. Except that it also blinds us to the full potential of sex and what it can offer us.

ORDINARY SEXISM

We like to consider the vagina as the female equivalent of the penis because penetration is a very effective way for the *man* to achieve orgasm. Why would we ever consider a sexual encounter to be anything other than a penis in a vagina? In patriarchal societies centred around men, the male experience of the world — including sex — is the only one that counts.

We believe it is the responsibility of the woman to adapt her sexuality in order to fit that of the man. And if he gets off by sticking his penis in her orifices, she should learn to get off that way, too!

Women are pressured to think they absolutely need a penis in order to climax.

During sex, a woman can achieve orgasm through various other acts (oral sex, fondling, fingering, and other simulation), but these are often perceived as secondary. They are less important. We call these acts "foreplay" and regard them as favours men accord women, and we rarely take them into account when tallying up the number of "real" sexual encounters we have experienced. A "real" sexual encounter is one considered "complete," consisting of a penis inserted into a vagina, followed by an in-and-out movement until ejaculation occurs.

NAIVE ROMANTICISM

The pro-vagina bias is also motivated by the idealized vision we have of sex: we desperately want sex to embody a perfect, balanced union between a man and a woman.

We want male and female sexualities to complement one another. The penis and the vagina fit together — how perfect! Isn't Mother Nature smart? Vaginal penetration stimulates the penis *and* the vagina, so we've got the best of both worlds!

Ah, how romantic. But in reality, heterosexual partners commonly experience an imbalance, beyond just how different the genital organs are when it comes to pleasure. Whether we want to or not, we have different preferences for pacing, frequency, timing, and intensity. Sex between a man and a woman can be just as seamless, or as mismatched, as sex between partners of the same gender.

Interestingly, lesbians experience orgasm more frequently than heterosexual and bisexual women. Below are the orgasm rates divided by sexual orientation according to a study of 6,151 participants conducted by the University of Indiana:[18]

Heterosexual man: 86 percent
Heterosexual woman: 62 percent

Bisexual man: 78 percent
Bisexual woman: 58 percent
Gay man: 85 percent
Lesbian: 75 percent

We can see that lesbians have fewer orgasms than both gay and straight men. Why is that? Perhaps since, as we have seen, the female orgasm is not as valued, not as sought after.

IS THE FEMALE ORGASM USEFUL?

Why do women orgasm? If climaxing is not directly related to reproduction, as is the case with male ejaculation, wouldn't that make it, by nature, nonessential? Would this explain why women make orgasming less of a priority than men do?

Noting this physiological difference between the sexes, researchers regularly question the pertinence of the female orgasm, which has been the subject of numerous hypotheses and studies.

For proponents of biology, let's look at a few studies that try to explain why, from an evolutionary perspective, the female orgasm exists, despite not being required for conception.

Researchers have recently speculated that the female orgasm may at one time have stimulated ovulation in mammals, thus contributing to reproduction.[19] According to Mihaela Pavličev and Günter Wagner, prolactin and oxytocin, two hormones that are released through orgasm, may have played a role in most mammals' ovulation around 60 million years ago. When ovulation became cyclic, as was the case for hominids and other species, the female orgasm ended up divorced from the reproductive process. At around the same time, the clitoris would have moved farther from the vagina, causing stimulation to become less assured during penetration.

While it is an interesting hypothesis, I can't help but notice that one of the researchers mentioned in an interview how the theory "might explain why *some women* achieve orgasm through masturbation or clitoral stimulation."[20] As if the issue were anecdotal. Yet this is how nine out of ten women climax! The pro-vagina bias appears to have convinced even researchers.

Montreal researcher Jim Pfaus brings up another theory concerning female pleasure: the clitoris may play a role in sex selection. It enables women to be more discerning when choosing the sexual partners who will later engage in penetration.

If a man manages to arouse a woman by stimulating her external sex organs, he is a good match. He has "proven his worth," has shown that he is attentive to the needs of his partner. She can be open to the idea of having a baby with him. Conversely, a man who does not sexually stimulate his partner, whether he is unable to or just lazy, proves that he will not be an attentive partner. And if this is the case, why risk conceiving a child with him?

According to this theory, the clitoris acts as a doorbell of sorts, allowing the woman to choose whether or not to let the man enter her vagina based on prior pleasure.

Whatever the Darwinian explanation, it is curious that the pertinence of female orgasm should come up as often as it does. We take for granted that the male orgasm has a reproductive function because it is tied to ejaculation, but this does not explain why, biologically speaking, ejaculation triggers the euphoria of orgasm. It would seem this is in order to motivate men to ejaculate as often as possible, increasing their chances to procreate. But men can ejaculate outside of a vagina — during masturbation, for instance. The male orgasm is not inherently linked to reproduction. Some might say that at the very least, the act of coming encourages men to head to the nearest vagina. But if that is the case, the orgasm as an incentive to seek out sexual contact would apply to women, as well.

AIM FOR THE GENITALS, MISS THE BRAIN

It is enough of a problem that there is a gendered gap when it comes to achieving orgasm in heterosexuals; that this gap has a negative impact on women's libidos adds insult to injury. It is frustrating to be aroused during sex without it resulting in orgasm. And if one partner orgasms, but not the other, it may lead to resentment that will hinder future relations, especially if the resentment persists.

The prospect of having sex without climaxing can diminish the desire to repeat the exercise. Conversely, experiencing pleasure promotes a person's sex drive. You could say that one orgasm leads to another.

And remember, it's much easier to come if the attraction was there initially. A woman who is not particularly attracted to a man *before* the encounter will find it difficult to reach orgasm *during* it. Trying to get a person of either gender to climax when they are not sexually aroused will prove much more difficult than if they are already burning with desire. It is likely we believe women take longer to climax than men do because there is a general lack of consideration for a woman's arousal prior to sex.

We often forget to take a woman's initial desire into account when studying the female orgasm. Our culture promotes the idea that women possess little spontaneous desire, and we have come to believe that the best method of arousing them is to stimulate their bodies. In this way we collectively ignore women's libidos, fail to provide them with enough sexual stimulation, and instead persuade ourselves that jump-starting their desire is just a question of touching their body in the right way.

It is pure denial that makes us — men and women alike — obsessed with the idea of finding the magic button on a woman's genitals that will trigger a rush of desire. It would be far more productive to stimulate a woman's desire on a daily basis before having sex, like we do with men, instead of trying to start from zero.

We also need to rethink the discourse encouraging women to "explore their bodies," a trademark of the sex-positive movement that positions sex as a healthy behaviour to promote. This trend allows us to talk about consent, among other things, and it is a movement I support. But when we compel women to explore their bodies we individualize the orgasm gap, which is really a social issue. Rather than explore the deeper reasons why women experience fewer orgasms than men, we act as if it were the fault of the individual. If a woman has a hard time climaxing, it is because she has not explored her body enough.

This injunction reaffirms the misleading idea that a woman's pleasure is complicated, that she must work hard and try different things in order to achieve this elusive thrill. Like a modern-day Christopher Columbus, a woman must set sail for a far-off and unknown land: her body. But most of the time women do know their bodies; we just infantilize (and mislead) them into thinking they haven't yet mastered the "right" way to experience pleasure.

In practice, this discourse takes on capitalist and sexist undertones that lure women toward practising BDSM (think *Fifty Shades of Grey*), buying sexy lingerie to heighten the mood, or engaging in anal sex, among other things. I use the word sexist because no one asks heterosexual men to explore their bodies. Nobody tells them to find ways of climaxing other than their penis. They aren't asked to submit to penetration, get battered about, or buy sexy clothes.

Of course when the pro-exploration discourse comes from advocates of the sex-positive movement, it is meant to be constructive. Most often it encourages women to try masturbation. But the orgasm gap will remain intact until we start wondering why women have less "spontaneous" desire to masturbate than men do.

By focusing on stimulating the body, we miss the real target: stimulating the brain.

I'll say it again: not every sexual interaction must involve both partners' quest for orgasm. It is possible to come away perfectly satisfied even without climaxing. Nevertheless, it is high time we reject the notion that the movement of a penis inside a vagina alone should bring a woman to climax. And the female orgasm is long overdue the same attention we give its male counterpart. Either that, or a man's orgasm should be just as optional as a woman's when procreation is not the goal.

Conclusion

Rethinking Sex to Liberate Women

> Grab them by the pussy.
> — President Donald J. Trump

Thinking about sex can be uncomfortable when we stop reducing it to pure biology. Things can get a little awkward once we admit sex is fundamentally a social activity.

Biology is obviously part of it; we seek out interpersonal contact to obtain physical pleasure, which may lead to reproduction in some instances. Yet the fact that humans search out and engage in this behaviour is just the tip of the iceberg. Sex is connected to a whole other world, one far removed from biology.

It is an organized system, one that defines how we establish, negotiate, and represent these contacts. It also prioritizes them.

Sex itself, along with the period of courtship that precedes it, is governed by rites and rituals. Similarly, we fuel and condition our desire through a collection of symbols.

Certain individuals, called "fetishists," will develop a sexual fascination with unconventional symbols related to their own personal history. But most of us will simply fall back on representations propagated by popular culture.

The reason porn is so predictable, the storylines written to feed our private fantasies so redundant, is that certain pervasive sex symbols have come to be so etched into our collective imagination that they have become essential for desire and, by extension, pleasure.

While overutilization of these symbols would constitute a cliché in some spheres, we consider them biologically pre-programmed when it comes to sex. In this way we can avoid asking uncomfortable questions.

But ultimately, they're still just clichés.

How women are passive and how we focus on their bodies, on youth, purity, and fashion — these are the most hackneyed sexual clichés. And stringing these clichés together reveals a matrix through which the cumshot principle emerges.

When we examine sexual stereotypes and how they impact our lives, we realize it is no coincidence that women and their bodies are placed at the centre of our fantasy world. It is wholly consistent with a woman's place within the world: on the fringes of power, on the second rung of the social ladder.

We are forced to admit that society prioritizes and normalizes heterosexual male desire. Women, on the other hand, are trained to give precedence to male sexual interest.

Female desire takes a back seat and women are expected to conform to a set of unspoken rules:

- They must let themselves be objectified by, and not objectify, men (the subjects).
- Their desire must follow, and be dependent on, a man's desire.
- They must display a distinct appearance and allure; women are like fireworks, sending off constant visual stimuli.
- They must prove pure and submissive in attitude (both as prey and in their quest for the Holy Grail of Love) and appearance (maintain a youthful aura).
- They must be seductive, always hinting at their potential to transform into a slut at the sight of a penis.
- And once a penis appears, they must try to climax through their vagina.

Women are asked to adapt their own desires to all of these fantasies projected onto them. We insist that they share these fantasies and forbid them to write their own scripts. Their job isn't to sully the man; it is to be sullied *by* him.

We think about and represent sex as a unidirectional force that originates with the man and is directed onto the woman. She is doomed to act as a target, a receptacle of desire. And that is the essence of the cumshot principle.

This is the dominant ideology. The resulting conventions include a purity imperative, a male hunter/female prey dynamic, sex segregation (which sanctions the mass objectification of women), an obsession with youthfulness, the subjectification of men, the Holy Grail of Love, and the pro-vagina bias. Together they establish an order and create a world where a woman's desire is formed around autophilia, where she must come to terms with rape culture, slut-shaming, a hyperawareness of the body — its imperfections, sex appeal, and decline — and all the contradictions these entail.

Sure, we can tell women they have the power to sexualize men and fight to change the system. But shifting the paradigm cannot rest on women's shoulders alone. It takes two to tango. Men are part of the problem — and also part of the solution.

The cumshot principle also alienates men by imposing certain rules onto them, such as being responsible for making the first move and dominating in the bedroom. The sexual potential of both genders is being held hostage by the status quo — the difference is that male desire forms the foundations of the system and supplies its raison d'être. Men desire sex, and our rituals serve to maintain and satisfy this desire. Female desire is oriented around and designed to achieve this imperative.

To do away with the cumshot principle, we need to eliminate the stereotypes it propagates. We need to give women the same political and economic power men have and let them produce their own set of cultural artifacts. Men must agree to be the object of female desire and use their own bodies to send visual stimuli. We must stop regarding sex as degrading and develop new sexual schemas that step beyond our Judeo-Christian past, ones that no longer hinge on guilt and impurity. We must restore integrity to the female body by ceasing to see it as offensive. We must work to make sex positive and put an end to sex segregation. Finally, we must break down and fuse the gendered silos where men and women remain trapped inside.

The clichés and practices fuelling the cumshot principle help perpetuate a coherent narrative. Their logic guides us, making it impossible for us to regard the world in any other way.

Female desire, unlike its male counterpart, cannot evolve independently within this context. It is secondary, optional, and unimportant.

The situation is grossly unfair.

It is tempting to view sex as one superficial element of women's liberation. But it is a truly fundamental issue, since the cumshot principle places submission at the heart of a woman's identity and domination at the heart of a man's.

By formatting women's desire, we are also formatting their personalities, dreams, and ambitions. And when we accord disproportionate attention to heterosexual male desire, we stand in the way of a woman's independence by limiting her potential outside of sex.

Many will disagree, arguing that our behaviours and desires are not a conduit for ideology, that what I am describing is strictly a biological matter, or that our relationship to sex is immutable because it is rooted in "human nature." That it's no use fighting the system. Many will brandish anecdotes that contradict the systemic phenomena I have described. I will be told the issue does not exist, and, in the same breath, that it cannot be avoided.

Like all unjust ideologies, the cumshot principle relies on effective propaganda to remain in place — propaganda that seeks to paint the status quo as unavoidable. The force of the propaganda reflects the weight of the issue.

And the stakes are high. Defying this ideology necessitates rethinking entire swathes of our social fabric. It would mean questioning the practices and symbols that give our lives meaning.

But if we truly want to achieve equality between men and women, we must do away with the cumshot principle and all the sexual stereotypes underpinning it. Because until we do, women will continue to get screwed.

THE CUMSHOT PRINCIPLE

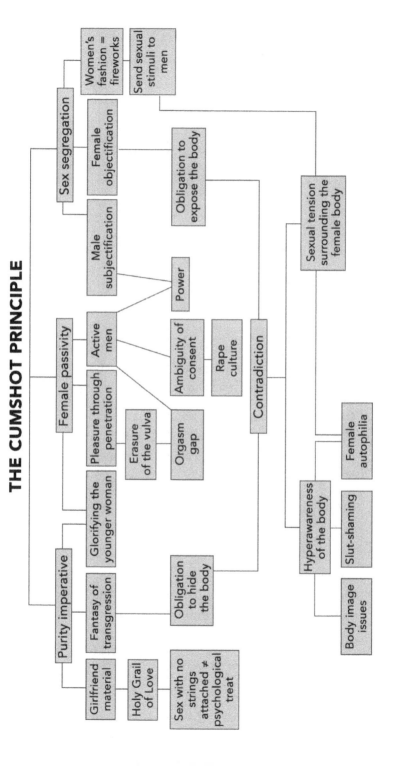

Glossary

Autophilia: love of one's own self (or of someone else onto whom we project ourselves).

Cumshot: in pornography, the final shot when a man ejaculates onto a woman's body. The cumshot principle is a result of the dominant ideology that defines desire as originating with the man and directed onto the woman.

Erasure of the vulva: cultural tendency to ignore a woman's external genitalia, which are frequently responsible for achieving orgasm.

Fantasy of transgression: sexual cliché rooted in religion that presents the idea of using sex to "sully" a presumably pure woman as exciting.

Girlfriend material: a woman deemed worthy of commitment, and thus worthy of being subjectified.

Heteronormativity: the notion that humanity is divided into two complementary sexes — man and woman — and that heterosexuality is the only acceptable sexual orientation.

Hollywood Age Gap: a trend in the film industry to pair actors over thirty-five with significantly younger actresses.

Holy Grail of Love: social conditioning that encourages women to prioritize the search for love.

Holy Grail of Sex: social conditioning that encourages men to prioritize the search for sex with multiple partners.

Hookup: occasional sexual interaction with no strings attached.

Hunter/prey dynamic: heterosexual courtship rituals establishing the man as active and the woman as passive.

Hyperawareness of body: a mental condition in women resulting from a collective obsession over their bodies that leads to body complexes, disproportionately links self-esteem to physical appearance, impedes a healthy sex life, and encourages autophilia.

Male gaze: creating cultural productions from a masculine, heterosexual perspective.

Objectification: process of reducing a human being to a body that is perceived as a tool to exploit.

Orgasm gap: how men experience a greater number of orgasms than women during sex.

Pro-vagina bias: cultural tendency to regard the vagina as the primary organ governing women's sexuality.

Psychological treat: reward gained from a situation by virtue of one's gender.

Purity imperative: cultural injunction requiring women to exude purity in attitude and appearance.

Rape culture: a set of beliefs, traditions, and representations that minimize, trivialize, or eroticize sexual assault.

Sex segregation: the practice of separating men and women.

Sexual revolution: the evolution of sexual mores in the West, between the mid-1960s and early 1970s.

Sexualization/eroticization: cultural process that assigns a sexual value to a part of the body.

Subjectification: process of acknowledging an individual by taking into account their personality, preferences, and desires.

Visual stimuli: symbols present in an individual's appearance or attitude that attract attention and are associated with desirability.

Notes

CHAPTER 1: ME HUNTER, YOU PREY

1. Paula England, "Understanding Hookup Culture: What's Really Happening on College Campuses," Media Education Foundation, 2011.
2. Eric R. Bressler, Rod A. Martin, and Sigal Balshine, "Production and Appreciation of Humor as Sexually Selected Traits," *Evolution and Human Behavior* 27, no. 2 (March 2006): 121–30.
3. The idea of everyday sexism refers to "words, actions, behaviours, or acts that exclude, marginalize, or belittle women," but are not perceived as such since they are part of the prevailing culture. Brigitte Grésy, *Petit traité contre le sexisme ordinaire* (Paris: Albin Michel, 2008).
4. Jeffrey A. Hall, "Sexual Selection and Humor in Courtship: A Case for Warmth and Extroversion," *Evolutionary Psychology* 13, no. 3 (2015).

5. John K. Donahue and Melanie C. Green, "A Good Story: Men's Storytelling Ability Affects Their Attractiveness and Perceived Status," *Personal Relationships* 23, no. 2 (June 2016): 199–213.

6. Amy Muise et al., "Not in the Mood? Men Under- (Not Over-) Perceive Their Partner's Sexual Desire in Established Intimate Relationships," *Journal of Personality and Social Psychology* 110, no. 5 (May 2016): 725–42.

7. Paul W. Eastwick and Eli J. Finkel, "Sex Differences in Mate Preferences Revisited: Do People Know What They Initially Desire in a Romantic Partner?," *Journal of Personality and Social Psychology* 94, no. 2 (February 2008): 245–64.

8. Mythical yet deeply entrenched diagnosis according to which women with a strong libido have a psychological disorder.

9. In Quebec, like elsewhere around the world, women and girls make up the majority of sexual assault victims. According to official police records from 2014, 84 percent of victims were female, while 96 percent of alleged offenders were male.

10. "Fais moi mal Johnny" is the title of a 1955 French song by Boris Vianin in which a woman sings of how she likes "rough sex," until one day her partner really beats her up. It has been criticized as a sexist song and was written by a man, but sung by a woman.

11. Lucia C. Lykke and Philip N. Cohen, "The Widening Gender Gap in Opposition to Pornography, 1975–2012," *Social Currents* (September 2015).

12. Daniel Bergner, *What Do Women Want? Adventures in the Science of Female Desire* (New York: Ecco, 2013).

CHAPTER 2: COUGARS AND NYMPHETS

1. Society still exerts control over the behaviour and appearance of mothers. In 2015, for instance, the *New York Post* asked people via Twitter whether they would let their mother out of the house dressed like celebrity moms Jennifer Lopez, Beyoncé, and Kim Kardashian.
2. Zoe Lawton and Paul Callister, "Older Women-Younger Men Relationships: The Social Phenomenon of 'Cougars,'" research notes, Institute of Policy Studies (January 2010).
3. The term "puma" can also be used to refer to a "younger" cougar — a woman in her thirties — or to a "cougar" over fifty. Although the term is broad, it will be used in this book to designate "men who date younger women"; after all, it's only fair to label men with unconventional sexual preferences, and not just women.
4. Stephen Follows, "Are Men in Romantic Movies Older Than Their Female Co-Stars?," *Film Data and Education,* June 2015, stephenfollows.com/are-men-in-romantic-films-older-than-women.
5. "The Hollywood Gender Age Gap: Part 1; Band of Brothers," *GraphJoy*, August 2015, graphjoy.com/2015/08/the-hollywood-gender-age-gap-part-1.
6. Stephen Addison, "'Cougar' Trend of Women Chasing Younger Men a Myth," Reuters, August 19, 2010.

7. Christian Rudder, "The Case for an Older Woman," OkCupid (blog), February 16, 2010, theblog.okcupid.com/the-case-for-an-older-woman-99d8cabacdf5.

8. Jean Twenge, "How Long Can You Wait to Have a Baby?," *The Atlantic* (July/August 2013).

9. Joan K. Morris and Eva Alberman, "Trends in Down's Syndrome Live Births and Antenatal Diagnoses in England and Wales from 1989 to 2008: Analysis of Data from the National Down Syndrome Cytogenetic Register," *British Medical Journal* 339 (2009): b3794.

10. M.V. Zaragoza et al., "Nondisjunction of Human Acrocentric Chromosomes: Studies of 432 Trisomic Foetuses and Liveborns," *Human Genetics* 94, no. 4 (October 1994): 411–17; H. Fisch et al., "The Influence of Paternal Age on Down Syndrome," *Journal of Urology* 169, no. 6 (June 2003): 2275–78.

11. World Health Organization, "Adolescent Pregnancy," Fact Sheet 364, updated January 2018 , apps.who.int/iris/bitstream/handle/10665/112320/WHO_;jsessionid=B54F92470BFF7D093982E639DFEC-6C1F?sequence=1.

12. This is similar to the parental investment theory, which holds that men, unlike women, don't need to be selective in choosing their sexual partner, because they won't be investing nine months of their life during the resulting gestation. It follows that men don't have to weigh the consequences of entering into a sexual relationship with a given partner.

13. Interview with Dr. Luc Bessette, "Forme physique, sexuelle, cognitive: à quel âge est-on à son apogée?," Radio-Canada, May 2015.

14. Laurie Tarkan, "The Biological Clock, Ticking for Men Too," *New York Times*, May 2, 2008.

15. Julia Medew, "Fertility Clock Ticks for Men Too," *Sydney Morning Herald*, March 26, 2012.

16. Interview with Dr. Luc Bessette.

17. *Sexplora*, Season 2, ICI Explora, 2017.

CHAPTER 3: THE PURITY IMPERATIVE

1. Demos, "The Use of Misogynistic Terms on Twitter," www.demos.co.uk/wp-content/uploads/2016/05/Misogyny-online.pdf.

2. Elizabeth A. Armstrong et al., "'Good Girls': Gender, Social Class, and Slut Discourse on Campus," *Social Psychology Quarterly* 77, no. 2 (May 2014).

3. Derek A. Kreager, "Unlike Boys, Girls Lose Friends for Having Sex, Gain Friends for Making Out," American Sociological Association, August 24, 2015, www.asanet.org/press-center/press-releases/unlike-boys-girls-lose-friends-having-sex-gain-friends-making-out.

4. To take this further: my suspicion is that many people are afraid that if their fantasies change, *nothing* will arouse them anymore. The result, they fear, would be some sort of sexual apocalypse.

CHAPTER 4: SEX SEGREGATION

1. Deuteronomy 22:5.

2. Antoine Krempf, "Les seins se porteraient mieux sans soutien-gorge," *France Info*, April 10, 2013, francetvInfo.fr/sciences/les-seins-se-porteraient mieux-sans-soutien-gorge_1651155.html). Krempf did qualify his results, allowing that the small sample size composed of athletes was not representative of the general population.

3. As women age, they often forgo long hair and form-fitting clothes: our culture condones, and even advocates, abandoning a classic image of femininity after a certain age.

4. American Society of Plastic Surgeons, "2015 Cosmetic Surgery Gender Distribution," *2015 Plastic Surgery Statistics Report* (2015): 10.

5. John Berger, *Ways of Seeing* (London: Penguin, 1972).

6. Laura Mulvey, "Visual Pleasure and Narrative Cinema," *Screen* 16, no. 3 (Fall 1975): 6–18.

7. Gerulf Rieger et al., "Sexual Arousal and Masculinity-Femininity in Women," *Journal of Personality and Social Psychology* 111, no. 2 (August 2016): 265–83.

8. Eleanor Steafel, "Women Are Either Bisexual or Gay But 'Never Straight,'" *Telegraph*, November 5, 2015, telegraph.co.uk/news/uknews/11977121/Women-are-either-bisexual-or-gay-but-never-straight.html.

CHAPTER 5: THE FIRST SEX

1. Philippe Bernard et al., "Integrating Sexual Objectification with Object Versus Person Recognition:

The Sexualized-Body-Inversion Hypothesis," *Psychological Science* 23 (2012), 469–71.

2. Naomi Wolf, *The Beauty Myth* (London, UK: Chatto & Windus, 1990), 139.

3. Paula England, "Understanding Hookup Culture," The Media Education Foundation, February 13, 2013, youtube.com/watch?v=L3Q2L7YQ2Hk.

CHAPTER 6: THE HOLY GRAIL

1. Geoffrey C. Urbaniak and Peter R. Kilmann, "Physical Attractiveness and the 'Nice Guy Paradox': Do Nice Guys Really Finish Last?," *Sex Roles* 49, no. 9–10 (November 2003): 413–26.

2. Pat Barclay, "Altruism as a Courtship Display: Some Effects of Third-Party Generosity on Audience Perceptions," *British Journal of Psychology* 101, no. 1 (February 2010): 123–35; Jerry M. Burger and Mica Cosby, "Do Women Prefer Dominant Men? The Case of the Missing Control Condition," *Journal of Research in Personality* 33 (1999): 358–68.

3. Moira Weigel, "The Foul Reign of the Biological Clock," *The Guardian*, May 10, 2016, theguardian .com/society/2016/may/10/foul-reign-of-the-biological-clock.

4. Conseil du statut de la femme, "Pour un partage équitable du congé parental," Government of Québec, April 2015, csf.gouv.qc.ca/wp-content/uploads/avis_partage_conge_parental.pdf.

5. C.L. Muehlenhard and S.K. Shippee, "Men's and Women's Reports of Pretending Orgasm," *Journal of Sex Research* 47, no. 6 (November 2010): 552–67.

6. The belief that a nuclear family headed by two heterosexual parents is the only acceptable model.

7. Terri D. Conley, Ali Ziegler, and Amy Moors, "Back lash from the Bedroom: Stigma Mediates Gender Differences in Acceptance of Casual Sex Offers," *Psychology of Women Quarterly* 37, no. 3 (2013).

8. "The Big One," *Gilmore Girls*, season 3, episode 16, written and produced by Amy Sherman-Palladino, aired February 23, 2003.

CHAPTER 7: THE ORGASM GAP

1. Mona Chalabi, "Gender Orgasm Gap," *FiveThirtyEight*, August 20, 2015, citing the National Survey of Sexual Health and Behavior Report (2009), fivethirtyeight.com/features/the-gender-orgasm-gap.

2. Paula England, "Understanding Hookup Culture."

3. Elizabeth A. Armstrong, Paula England, and Alison C.K. Fogarty, "Accounting for Women's Orgasm and Sexual Enjoyment in College Hookups and Relationships," *American Sociological Review* 77, no. 3 (May 2012).

4. Jessica R. Wood et al., "Was It Good for You Too?: An Analysis of Gender Differences in Oral Sex Practices and Pleasure Ratings Among Heterosexual Canadian University Students," *Canadian Journal of Human Sexuality* 25, no. 1 (2016).

5. Elizabeth A. Armstrong, Paula England, and Alison C.K. Fogarty, "Accounting for Women's Orgasm and Sexual Enjoyment in College Hookups

and Relationships"; Barbara J. Risman and Virginia Rutter, *Families As They Really Are* (New York: W.W. Norton, 2009), 362–77.

6. Elisabeth A. Lloyd, *The Case of the Female Orgasm: Bias in the Science of Evolution* (Cambridge: Harvard University Press, 2006).

7. "Lili Against the Machine," *Sexplora*, Season 1, ICI Explora, *YouTube*, January 13, 2016, youtube.com/watch?v=S5yIpGM0gsU.

8. Elisabeth A. Lloyd, *The Case of the Female Orgasm.*

9. Annie Sautivet, "État des lieux des connaissances, représentations et pratiques sexuelles des jeunes adolescents," sexology thesis, Université Montpellier I (2009).

10. Breanne Fahs and Elena Frank, "Notes from the Back Room: Gender, Power, and (In)visibility in Women's Experiences of Masturbation," *Journal of Sex Research* 51, no. 3 (2014): 241–52.

11. Cécile Daumas, "Vaginale/clitoridienne. À corps et à cris," *Libération*, August 2, 2008, liberation.fr/cahier-special/2008/08/02/vaginale-clitoridienne-a-corps-et-a-cris_77436.

12. Letitia Glocer Firoini and Graciela Abelin-Sas Rose, eds., *On Freud's "Femininity"* (London: Routledge, 2011).

13. Stuart Brody and Rui Miguel Costa, "Vaginal Orgasm Is Associated with Less Use of Immature Psychological Defense Mechanisms," *Journal of Sexual Medicine* 5, no. 5 (March 2008): 167–76.

14. Nicole Prause et al., "Clitorally Stimulated Orgasms Are Associated with Better Control of Sexual Desire,

and Not Associated with Depression or Anxiety, Compared with Vaginally Stimulated Orgasms," *Journal of Sexual Medicine* 13, no. 11 (September 2016): 1676–85.

15. Vincenzo Puppo and Giulia Puppo, "Anatomy and Physiology of the Clitoris, Vestibular Bulbs, and Labia Minora with a Review of the Female Orgasm and the Prevention of Female Sexual Dysfunction," *Clinical Anatomy* 26, no. 1 (January 2013): 134–52.

16. James G. Pfaus et al., "The Whole Versus the Sum of Some of the Parts: Toward Resolving the Apparent Controversy of Clitoral Versus Vaginal Orgasms," *Socioaffective Neuroscience & Psychology* 6, no. 1 (October 2016).

17. Diana Fleischman, Daniel Fessler, and Argine Cholakians, "Testing the Affiliation Hypothesis of Homoerotic Motivation in Humans: The Effects of Progesterone and Priming," *Archives of Sexual Behavior* 44, no. 5 (July 2015): 1395–1404.

18. Justin R. Garcia et al., "Variation in Orgasm Occurrence by Sexual Orientation in a Sample of U.S. Singles," *Journal of Sexual Medicine* 11, no. 11 (November 2014): 2645–52.

19. Mihaela Pavličev and Günter Wagner, "The Evolutionary Origin of Female Orgasm," *Journal of Experimental Zoology* 326, no. 6 (July 2016): 326–37.

20. Günter Wagner, quoted in Agence France-Presse, "L'orgasme féminin, un vestige de l'évolution?," August 2, 2016. My emphasis.

Single Girl Problems
Andrea Bain

"If one more person tells me about their third cousin twice removed who met the love of their life online, I'm going to take out my weave and eat it."

Being single sucks! Well, that's what everyone says, anyway. Single women over the age of 29 are seen as lonely, miserable, undesirable, and cat-crazy. Family members, friends — heck, even perfect strangers ask, "When are you going to get married?" This book flips the script on what it means to be a single woman in the twenty-first century. With dating horror story anecdotes and advice about online dating, self-esteem, sex, money, and freezing your eggs, Andrea Bain takes the edge off being single and encourages women to never settle.

BREAKING THE CURSE
OF MENSTRUATION

AMANDA LAIRD

Heavy Flow
Amanda Laird

What do you know about your menstrual cycle?

Your menstrual cycle is your fifth vital sign — a barometer of health and wellness that is as telling as your pulse or blood pressure. Yet most of us see our periods as nothing more than a source of inconvenience, shame, and stigma.

The reasons for this are vast and complex and many are rooted in misogyny. The fact is, women around the world are taught the bare minimum about menstruation, and the messages they do receive are negative: that periods are painful and gross, turn us into hormonal messes, and shouldn't be discussed.

By examining the history of period shame and stigma and its effects on women's health and wellness today, and providing a crash course in menstrual self-care, *Heavy Flow* aims to lift the veil on menstruation, change the narrative, and break the "curse" once and for all.

Book Credits
Project Editor: Jenny McWha
Copy Editor: Shannon Whibbs
Proofreader: Shari Rutherford

Cover and Interior Designer: Laura Boyle

Publicist: Elham Ali

Dundurn
Publisher: J. Kirk Howard
Vice-President: Carl A. Brand
Editorial Director: Kathryn Lane
Artistic Director: Laura Boyle
Production Manager: Rudi Garcia
Publicity Manager: Michelle Melski
Manager, Accounting and Technical Services: Livio Copetti

Editorial: Allison Hirst, Dominic Farrell, Jenny McWha,
Rachel Spence, Elena Radic, Melissa Kawaguchi
Marketing and Publicity: Kendra Martin, Elham Ali,
Tabassum Siddiqui, Heather McLeod
Design and Production: Sophie Paas-Lang

dundurn.com   dundurnpress
@dundurnpress   dundurnpress
dundurnpress   info@dundurn.com

FIND US ON NETGALLEY & GOODREADS TOO!

DUNDURN